Verbal Reasoning

Siân Goodspeed

Name *Aidan Malhotra*

Schofield & Sims

Introduction

Verbal reasoning is language-based problem solving. It involves thinking about words, letters, patterns and **sequences**. Verbal reasoning skills are useful for school tests, such as the 11+. There are many types of verbal reasoning question – covering, for example, spelling, word meanings, maths and code-breaking. The question types in this book are among the most common. Verbal reasoning skills are important in other aspects of life too. Practising these skills expands your **vocabulary**, improves your spelling and develops your ability to use **logic**.

How to use this book

Before you start using this book, write your name in the box on the first page. Then decide how to begin. If you want a complete course on verbal reasoning, work right through the book. Another way to use the book is to dip into it when you want to find out about a particular type of question. The contents page or the index will help you to find the pages you need. Whichever way you choose, don't do too much at once – it's better to work in short bursts.

When you are ready to begin, find some scrap paper – or ask an adult for some. You may find this useful for your workings out. As you make a start, look out for these icons, which mark different parts of the text.

Explanation
This text explains key points about the question type and gives examples. Read it before you start the activities. Words shown like **this** appear in the combined index and glossary (page 88). The glossary focuses on terms used to explain reasoning questions. To understand other terms, you may need to refer to **Understanding English** or **Understanding Maths**.

Hint
This text gives you extra information on how you might tackle a particular activity.

Activities
These are the activities that you should complete. Usually you write your answer in the space provided. **After you have worked through all the activities on a page, turn to pages 70 to 86 to check your answers. Where appropriate, these pages explain how each correct answer is reached. Read them carefully.** When you are sure that you understand a question type, tick the box beside it on the Contents page.

Important
This text tells you something that you must remember if you want your answers to be correct.

Contents

Tick the box when you have worked through the topic.

Here you are given a **series** of letters. You need to look for a pattern and find the next two letters. An alphabet is given to help you.

A B C D E F G H I J K L M N O P Q R S T U V W X Y Z

For example: SW UY WA YC AE (?)

- Look at the first letters of each pair. Count the jumps between them. For example, there are two jumps in the alphabet between **S** and **U**.

- Write the numbers above the **sequence**. This makes it easier to spot a pattern. Use **+** for forwards jumps. Use **–** for backwards jumps.

- Do the same for the second letters of each pair. Count the jumps. Write the numbers.

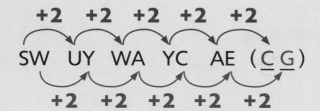

Answer: C G

When you have found the pattern you can write the final pair of numbers.

Look out for different types of patterns when solving letter sequences.

Forwards and backwards movements

For example: PT MV JX GZ DB (?)

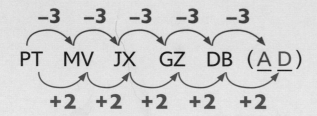

Answer: A D

The jumps go backwards from one letter and forwards from the other

Find the next two letters. The alphabet above will help you.

1. JP KR LT MV NX (I Y)   **3.** ZA YB XC WD VE (U F)

2. QE NH KK HN EQ (K K)   **4.** FF HE JD LC NB (O G)

> **Hint** If you are **jumping forwards** and you reach **Z** with more letters to go, carry on from **A** again. Count **Z** to **A** as one step. If you are **jumping backwards** from **A**, go to **Z**. This too counts as one step. It may help if you add three or four letters to either end of the alphabet, like this:
>
> W X Y Z A B C D E F G H I J K L M N O P Q R S T U V W X Y Z A B C D

Here are two other pattern types to look out for.

Increasing or decreasing gaps

+0 +1 +2 +3 +4

SS SW TZ VB YC (CC)

+4 +3 +2 +1 +0

Answer: CC

Here, the number of letters in a jump **increases** between the **first** letters of each pair. It **decreases** between the **second** letters.

Alternating gaps

+3 +5 +3 +5 +3

EC HF MK PN US (XV)

+3 +5 +3 +5 +3

Answer: XV

Sometimes, the gaps **alternate**. They go **in turns** between three jumps and five jumps.

Find the next two letters in the series. Use the alphabet on page 4 to help you.

1. MO PR QS TV UW (Y X)

2. TU YZ CD FG HI (JK)

3. QP OO NM LL KJ (___)

4. HJ GK EM BP XT (___)

Leapfrogging

If there are more than eight jumps between letters or if they seem to follow no pattern, look for **two** patterns that **leapfrog** over each other.

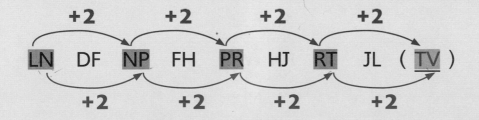

+2   +2   +2   +2

LN DF NP FH PR HJ RT JL (TV)

+2   +2   +2   +2

Answer: TV

With leapfrogging sequences, always make sure you jump over the last pair of letters to get to the answer.

Use the alphabet to find the next two letters in the series.

5. AC SU DF VX GI YA (___)

6. PO DC ML BA JI ZY (___)

7. RO FD SP GE UR IG XU LJ (___)

8. PT DC OS FE LP GF KO IH (___)

Hint Learn to continue the alphabet from any point. Knowing it backwards will help too.

Letter codes

Here you work out how two pairs of letters are connected. Then you find the pair of letters that go with a third pair of letters in the same way.

For example: BE is to **YV** as **GJ** is to (?)

There are two ways of solving letter code questions.

Letter partners

- Every letter in the first half of the alphabet has a partner in the second half. You draw a line down the centre of the alphabet given, between **M** and **N**. Then you number it as shown below.

A B C D E F G H I J K L M | N O P Q R S T U V W X Y Z
1 2 3 4 5 6 7 8 9 10 11 12 13 | 13 12 11 10 9 8 7 6 5 4 3 2 1

- Any two letters with the same number under them are partners. For example, **A** and **Z** are both numbered **1** and are partners. This is sometimes called the **mirror technique**. Each letter's partner is reflected in the central line.

Find the letter partner of each of the following. Use the alphabet above to help you.

1. B Y ✓
2. L O ✓
3. G T ✓
4. U F ✓
5. O L ✓
6. S H ✓

7. I R ✓
8. X C ✓
9. E V ✓
10. W D ✓
11. N M ✓
12. K P ✓

Hint Learn the partner of each letter of the alphabet (**A** goes with **Z**, **B** goes with **Y**, and so on). This helps you to spot letter partner questions quickly.

Letter codes

Now work through the **Letter partners** question at the top of page 6.

BE is to **YV** as **GJ** is to **(?)**

(2,5) (5,2) 7,10 (10,7)

- Look at the first pair of letters. Check whether their partners are in the second pair.

A	B	C	D	E	F	G	H	I	J	K	L	M	N	O	P	Q	R	S	T	U	V	W	X	Y	Z
1	2	3	4	5	6	7	8	9	10	11	12	13	13	12	11	10	9	8	7	6	5	4	3	2	1

- **B** has **2** under it. So does **Y**. So **B** and **Y** are partners. **E** and **V** both have **5** under them, so they are partners too. So this is a **Letter partners** question.

- Find the partners of each of the letters in the third pair, **GJ**, by looking at the other half of the alphabet.

- **G = 7**. The other letter with a **7** under it is **T**.

- **J = 10**. The other letter with a **10** under it is **Q**.

Answer: TQ

> Sometimes the first and second letters of each pair are reversed, for example:
> **BE** (2, 5) is to **VY** (5, 2) as **GJ** (7, 10) is to (**?**) **Answer: QT** (10, 7).

A	B	C	D	E	F	G	H	I	J	K	L	M	N	O	P	Q	R	S	T	U	V	W	X	Y	Z
1	2	3	4	5	6	7	8	9	10	11	12	13	13	12	11	10	9	8	7	6	5	4	3	2	1

Find the letters that complete the sentence in the best way. Use the alphabet to help you.

1. LF is to OU as RS is to __HI__

2. PR is to KI as VX is to __CE__

3. CB is to YX as LP is to __KO__

4. HE is to VS as UZ is to __AF__

5. MO is to NL as RD is to ~~~~ DR IW

6. AJ is to QZ as KL is to __OP__

Letter codes

Jumping

For example: CX is to DW as HS is to (?)

- Check to see if this is a **Letter partners** question (see pages 6 and 7).

- If it is not, it is a **Jumping** question.
  Write the **first** pair of letters above the **second** pair:

  CX
  DW

- Count the jumps from the top letter to the one below.
  Use **+** for forwards and **–** for backwards jumps.
  First count **C** to **D**, then **X** to **W**.

- Look at the pink arrows. The first letter jumps forwards by **1**. The second letter jumps backwards by **1**.

- Now apply the same number of jumps (**+1** then **–1**) to the third pair, **HS**.
  Look at the blue arrows. **H + 1** is **I** and **S – 1** is **R**.

Answer: IR

1. CE is to FH as DF is to ___
2. LO is to JM as PS is to _____
3. DD is to GB as JJ is to _____
4. MS is to RW as DH is to _____
5. SU is to KM as WZ is to _____
6. EC is to JX as OM is to _____
7. CT is to KR as NJ is to _____
8. LW is to IA as PZ is to _____

Word codes

Word codes are similar to letter codes. You are given a word and have to find the code, or you are given a code and have to work out the word.

Letter partners – find the code

For example: If the code for **CRAB** is **XIZY**, what is the code for **FISH**?

A	B	C	D	E	F	G	H	I	J	K	L	M	N	O	P	Q	R	S	T	U	V	W	X	Y	Z
1	2	3	4	5	6	7	8	9	10	11	12	13	13	12	11	10	9	8	7	6	5	4	3	2	1

- Number the alphabet. Is this a **Letter partners** question? The first letter in CRAB is partners with the first letter in the code XIZY. **C** = 3 and **X** = 3, so they are partners.

- Check the other letters in CRAB and XIZY. **R** = 9 and **I** = 9, **A** = 1 and **Z** = 1, **B** = 2 and **Y** = 2. They are all partners. This is a **Letter partners** question.

- Now use the alphabet to work out the code for FISH.

F = 6	**I** = 9	**S** = 8	**H** = 8	**Answer:**
The other letter numbered 6 is **U**. So **U** is the code letter for **F**.	The other letter numbered 9 is **R**. So **R** is the code letter for **I**.	**H** = 8 too, so **H** is the code letter for **S**.	**S** = 8 too, so **S** is the code letter for **H**.	**URHS**

Use the alphabet to help you answer the following.

1. If the code for SHEEP is HSVVK, what is the code for COWS? _XLDH_

2. If the code for DANCE is WZMXV, what is the code for SING? _HRMT_

3. If TRAIN is written in code as GIZRM,

what is the code for COACH? _XLZXS_

4. If HORSE in code is SLIHV, what is the code for PONY? _KLMB_

5. If the code for HAPPY is SZKKB, what is the code for ANGRY? _ZMTIB_

6. If ANIMAL is written in code as ZMRNZO,

what is the code for INSECT? _RMHVXG_

Letter partners – find the word

A B C D E F G H I J K L M | N O P Q R S T U V W X Y Z
1 2 3 4 5 6 7 8 9 10 11 12 13 | 13 12 11 10 9 8 7 6 5 4 3 2 1

For example: If the code for **STAR** is **HGZI**, what does **NLLM** mean?

- Number the alphabet. Is this a **Letter partners** question (see page 9)?
- The **S** in STAR is partners with the **H** in HGZI. The other letters are partners too. So this is a **Letter partners** question.
- Now find the partner for each letter in the code NLLM.
  N = 13 and **M** = 13, so the first letter of the word is **M**.
  L is partners with **O** and **M** is partners with **N**.

Answer: MOON

Hint You number the alphabet to see which letters are partners. Instead of numbering you can write the first half of the alphabet backwards under the second half. This too helps you see which letters are partners.

A B C D E F G H I J K L M | N O P Q R S T U V W X Y Z
M L K J I H G F E D C B A

1. If the code for FARM is UZIN, what does BZIW mean? _____

2. If NIGHT is written in code as MRTSG, what does WZIP mean? _____

3. If HOVVK is the code for SLEEP, what does WIVZN mean? _____

4. If NLMPVB in code means MONKEY,

what does TRIZUUV mean? _____

5. If PILOT is written in code as KROLG, what does KOZMV mean? _____

6. If the code for UNDER is FMWVI, what does ZYLFG mean? _____

Word codes

Jumping – find the code

If the question is not a **Letter partners** question, use the **Jumping** technique, as with the **Letter codes**.

For example: If the code for **SAND** is **UCPF**, what is the code for **SEA**?

- Check to see if it is a **Letter partners** question (see page 9). It is not.
- It is a **Jumping** question (see page 8). You are looking for a **code**. Write the **first code**. Then write the **first word** above the **code**:

SAND

UCPF

- Count the jumps from the top letter to the one below. Use **+** for forwards and **–** for backwards jumps. Count **S** to **U**, then work through the other letters.

- Look at the pink arrows and numbers. Each letter jumps forwards by 2.
- Now apply the same number of jumps (+2) to the third item in the question, **SEA**. Look at the blue arrows.

S + 2 = U

E + 2 = G

A + 2 = C

Answer: UGC

1. If the code for BLUE is CMVF, what is the code for GREEN? _____

2. If KNTC is the code for LOUD, what is the code for QUIET? _____

3. If the code for GRASS is HTDWX, what is the code for TREE? _____

4. If PARTY is written in code as OWQPX,

   what is the code for FEAST? _____

5. If the code for HISTORY is KHVSRQB,

   what is the code for SCIENCE? _____

6. If LORRY is written in code as OJWMD,

   what is the code for TRUCK? _____

Word codes

Jumping – find the word

For example: If the code for **SHOE** is **TJRI**, what does **TQFO** mean?

- Is this a **Letter partners** question (see pages 9 and 10)? It is not.

- It is a **Jumping** question (see pages 8 and 11). You are looking for a **word**. Write the **first word**. Then write the **first code** above the **word**.

  TJRI

  SHOE

- Count the jumps from the top letter to the one below. Use **+** for forwards and **–** for backwards jumps. Count **T** to **S**, then work through the other letters.

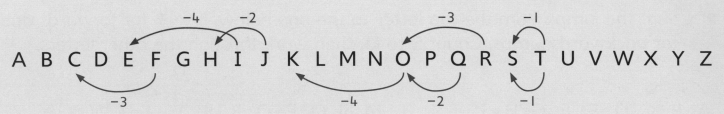

| T to S = –1 | R to O = –3 | TJRI |
| J to H = –2 | I to E = –4 | SHOE |

- Look at the pink arrows. Each letter jumps backwards – by 1, then 2, then 3, then 4.

- Apply the same jumps to the third item, **TQFO**. Look at the blue arrows.

| T – 1 = S | F – 3 = C | TQFO |
| Q – 2 = O | O – 4 = K | SOCK |

Answer: SOCK

1. If TREE in code is USFF, what does CVTI mean? _____

2. If the code for WALK is XCOO, what does SWQ mean? _____

3. If JCPM means LARK in code, what does EWJN mean? _____

4. If WORK is written in code as ZRUN, what does SODB mean? _____

5. If the code for MOTHER is LMQDZL, what does RGPPZL mean? _____

6. If WHISPER is written in code as YGKRRDT,

   what does NZWFJSGQ mean? _____

Hint   To find a **code**, write the **first code**, then write the **first word** above it.

To find a **word**, write the **first word**, then write the **first code** above it.

Match the codes

You are given four words and three number codes. Each code goes with one of the words. The same numbers represent the same letters in all of them. One code is missing.

For example:

R A I L   M E A L   R A I N   M A I L
    7 3 5 1   2 3 5 8   7 9 3 1

- First, work out which code goes with which word.
- Look for letters that the words have **in common**. Look for numbers that the codes have in common. Start with the letters at the end or the beginning of the words.
- Once you have matched a number to a letter, write the number above all the same letters.

Three of the words end in **L** and two of the codes end in **1**. So **L** is represented by **1**. You can write it in.

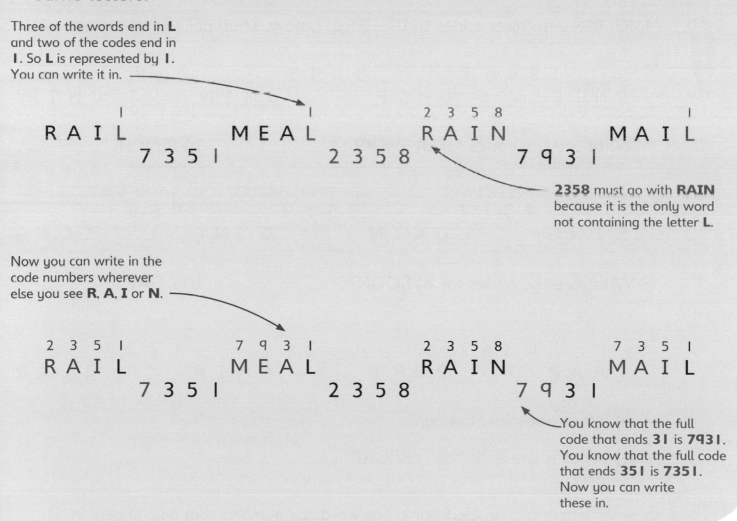

2358 must go with **RAIN** because it is the only word not containing the letter **L**.

Now you can write in the code numbers wherever else you see **R, A, I** or **N**.

You know that the full code that ends **31** is **7931**. You know that the full code that ends **351** is **7351**. Now you can write these in.

Match the codes

Now you can answer the questions below.

```
 2 3 5 1          7 9 3 1          2 3 5 8          7 3 5 1
 R A I L          M E A L          R A I N          M A I L
      7 3 5 1          2 3 5 8          7 9 3 1
```

a) What is the code for **MANE**?
Look at the number above each of these letters.
M is **7**, **A** is **3**, **N** is **8** and **E** is **9**.

Answer: 7389

b) What does **7511** mean?
Look at the letter below each of these numbers. **7** is **M**, **5** is **I** and **1** is **L**.

Answer: MILL

Match these number codes to the words below. Then answer the questions.

1.
```
      8 4 6 7          3 4 9 5          8 4 9 7
  S H I P          C H O P          S H I N          C H I P
```

What are the codes for **a)** SHOP? _____   **b)** PINCH? _____

2.
```
      9 5 1 7          3 5 1 9          9 8 4 1
  S I N G          G A I N          G O N E          S O N G
```

What are the codes for **a)** SOON? _____   **b)** AGAIN? _____

3.
```
      4 3 6 2          4 5 2 1          1 7 3 2
  T R A P          P O R T          P A I R          T E A R
```

a) What does 4321 mean?   _____

b) What is the code for TERROR?   _____

> **Hint** Look for letters that only appear in one word and numbers that only appear in one code.

You are given two pairs of words and a question word. In each pair, the second word is made using some of the letters in the first word. The position of the letters is the same for both pairs.

You work out the position of the second word within the first word. Then you find the letters that are in the same position in the question word. You make a word from them.

Working from left to right

In these questions the second words are easy to spot. Look at the first pair of words. Find the pattern.

For example: (mask ask)   (band and)   (stop [?])

ask is made from **mask** by dropping the first letter

and is made by dropping the first letter of **band**

to find the answer, drop the **s** in **stop**

Answer: top

Letters may be added to or removed from any position, not just the beginning or end of the word.

1. (pant pan)   (band ban)   (scom _____)

2. (tram ram)   (twin win)   (boat _____)

3. (hop shop)   (aid said)   (ash _____)

4. (many man)   (seed see)   (lady _____)

5. (all ball)   (ore pore)   (ear _____)

6. (grown gown)   (steal seal)   (black _____)

7. (table tale)   (tire tie)   (bleed _____)

8. (grain rain)   (tread read)   (cloud _____)

9. (bend bed)   (sand sad)   (burn _____)

10. (tramp trap)   (grind grid)   (beard _____)

Make a word from one other word

Taking letters from any position

These questions involve taking letters from any position in the first word to make the second word. The letters may not necessarily be used in the same order as in the first word.

For example: (brings gin) (shield lie) (glares [?])

Number the letters in **brings**.

Then number the letters in the word **gin** according to their position in the word **brings**.

If you have found a pattern in the first pair of words, do not bother with the second pair. Notice that this pair has exactly the same pattern as the first.

```
1 2 3 4 5 6   5 3 4      1 2 3 4 5 6   5 3 4      1 2 3 4 5 6   5 3 4
(b r i n g s   g i n)    (s h i e l d   l i e)    (g l a r e s   e a r)
```

Number the letters in **glares**.

Take the letters from the same position as in the earlier pairs (534). 5 = **e**, 3 = **a**, 4 = **r**.

Answer: <u>ear</u>

Hint The second set of words always follows the same pattern as the first set.

1. (party trap) (stare rats) (liver _____)

2. (tinsel lint) (leaded deal) (denies _____)

3. (amused muse) (staked take) (phoned _____)

4. (crawls law) (growls low) (tootle _____)

5. (please slap) (treads drat) (brought _____)

6. (around ran) (apart pat) (abound _____)

7. (trail rat) (though hot) (troop _____)

8. (ground rod) (spoilt pot) (stolen _____)

9. (ambush ham) (inward din) (aghast _____)

10. (adrift rift) (entail tail) (appear _____)

Make a word from one other word

Words with repeated letters

Sometimes, one or more of the letters in the second word are found in more than one place in the first word.

For example: (classes sale)   (hounds duos)   (blurred [?])

Number the letters in **classes**.

Number the letters in the word **sale** according to their position in **classes**.

s appears three times. Write all three numbers above the **s**.

Number the second pair in the same way. Notice that the first letter of the second word is taken from position 5 (not 4 or 7) because that is the position of the letter **d** in **hounds**.

```
                4
                5
1 2 3 4 5 6 7   7 3 2 6      1 2 3 4 5 6   5 3 2 6      1 2 3 4 5 6 7   5 3 2 6
(c l a s s e s   s a l e)    (h o u n d s   d u o s)    (b l u r r e d   r u l e)
```

Number the letters in **blurred**.

Take the letters from positions 5326.
5 = r, 3 = u, 2 = l, 6 = e.

Answer: rule

1. (bellow low)   (maggot got)   (barrow _____)

2. (juggle leg)   (muddle led)   (window _____)

3. (proper pope)   (weaker wake)   (fronds _____)

4. (stones nest)   (stewed west)   (deacon _____)

5. (dribble bile)   (bramble bale)   (whistle _____)

6. (asleep pale)   (haunts shun)   (instil _____)

7. (bottle lot)   (middle lid)   (toggle _____)

8. (doted dot)   (metal let)   (timed _____)

9. (dented dent)   (forest tore)   (lunged _____)

10. (denote teen)   (handle lean)   (galore _____)

Make a word from two other words

Taking letters from any position

Here the word in the middle of the first group is made using letters from the words on either side. Work out the position of the letters in the first group. Then make a word using the letters in the same positions in the second group.

For example: (speak [spin] wine)   (train [?] ripe)

Look at the middle word, **spin**. **Identify** where each letter is found in **speak** and **wine**. Point at the letter in the middle word of the first group and then to its **location** in the words either side. As you find each letter, go straight to the second group. Find the letter in the same position. Write the letters as you go.

The first letter of **spin** is found at the beginning of **speak**, so the missing word begins with the first letter of **train**, **t**.

(speak [spin] wine)   (train [tr___] ripe)

The second letter of **spin** is found in the second position in **speak**. So the second letter in the missing word is the second letter in the word **train**, **r**.

The third letter of **spin** is found in the second position in **wine**. So the third letter in the missing word is the second letter in the word **ripe**, **i**.

(speak [spin] wine)   (train [trip] ripe)

The last letter of **spin** is found in the third position in **wine**. So the last letter in the missing word is the third letter in the word **ripe**, **p**.

Answer: trip

1. (help [hear] pair)   (soup [_____] grit)

2. (night [this] sulk)   (cream [_____] entry)

3. (magic [aged] mode)   (lever [_____] line)

4. (shop [save] vane)   (pace [_____] alone)

5. (sound [done] lake)   (peels [_____] leaf)

6. (shower [wash] army)   (thumb [_____] open)

7. (hand [hint] site)   (lash [_____] moth)

8. (drop [dear] vase)   (clap [_____] halo)

Make a word from two other words

Words with repeated letters

Sometimes, one or more of the letters in the middle word can be found in more than one location in the outside words.

For example: (temple [pine] into)   (frothy [?] easy)

The first letter in **pine** comes from the fourth letter in **temple, p**. So the first letter of the missing word comes from the fourth letter in **froth, t**.

(temple [pine] into)   (frothy [te___] easy)

The second letter in **pine** is the first letter of **into**, so the second letter of the missing word is **e**.

The third letter in **pine** is from the second letter in **into**, so the next missing letter is **a**.

tear

(temple [pine] into)   (frothy [teay] easy)

The last letter in **pine** is in the second **and** the sixth positions in the word **temple**. So look at the second and sixth letters in the word **frothy, r** and **y**. Write one of the letters above the other to make two words. Decide which is a real word.

> **!** If you are doing a multiple choice paper and you come across alternative answers, check which option appears on the answer sheet.

Answer: <u>tear</u> (because **teay** is not a word)

> **!** There may be several repeated letters. You must write down **all** the letter options.

1. (melt [test] spot)   (leap [_____] rink)

2. (drop [rope] plea)   (them [_____] arts)

3. (rush [husk] risk)   (leer [_____] pain)

4. (need [dens] soup)   (nets [_____] time)

5. (rattle [right] sigh)   (hanger [_____] hero)

6. (balloon [lands] skid)   (hobbles [_____] yams)

Now test your skills with these practice pages. If you get stuck, go back to pages 4 to 19 for some reminders.

The hint on page 12 will be especially helpful when you answer the **Word codes** questions opposite.

Letter sequences

Using the alphabet to help you, find the next pair of letters in the **sequence**.

A B C D E F G H I J K L M N O P Q R S T U V W X Y Z

1. BD CE DF EG FH _____

2. LK NM PO RQ TS _____

3. JL HI FF DC BZ _____

4. VE UF TG SH RI _____

5. DL EM GO JR NV _____

6. AE WX CG YZ EI AB GK _____

Letter codes

Using the alphabet to help you, find the letters that complete each sentence.

A B C D E F G H I J K L M N O P Q R S T U V W X Y Z

7. AC is to DF as HJ is to _____

8. SA is to ZH as MP is to _____

9. CD is to XW as EF is to _____

10. GJ is to IL as RU is to _____

11. OQ is to RP as WV is to _____

12. HB is to YS as PL is to _____

Word codes

Using the alphabet to help you, work out the code or word for each question below.

A B C D E F G H I J K L M N O P Q R S T U V W X Y Z

1. If the code for APPLE is CQRMG,

   what is the code for ORANGE? _____

2. If DRAGON is written in code as CQZFNM,

   how would KNIGHT be written? _____

3. If KFWWOV means PUDDLE in code,

   what does WIRAAOV mean? _____

4. If the code for MELON is NGOSS, what does MGPSS mean? _____

5. If MOUNTAIN is coded as NLFMGZRM,

   what is the code for VALLEY? _____

6. If the code for PLANT is KOZMG,

   what is the code for ANIMAL? _____

Match the codes

Match the codes to the words then answer the questions that follow.

7.   1 4 8 7   3 4 6 3   3 4 5 1
   T H I S   T H A T   S H O W   W H A T

   a) What is the code for THIS? _____

   b) What is the code for THAW? _____

   c) What does 7614 mean? _____

8.   9 1 3 6   6 8 9 1   6 8 7 3
   M O S T   S T E M   D O E S   M O D E

   a) What is the code for STEM? _____

   b) What is the code for MOODS? _____

   c) What does 93379 mean? _____

Make a word from one other word

In these questions there are three pairs of words.
The third pair of words are made in the same way as the first two pairs.
Find the missing word and write it on the line.

1. (west wet)   (best bet)   (fast ___gat___)

2. (chain chin)   (grain grin)   (breed ___~~braid~~ bred___)

3. (waddle lad)   (little lit)   (meddle _____)

4. (matron tram)   (poster stop)   (masher _____)

5. (rampart ramp)   (lantern rant)   (mentors _____)

6. (assures sure)   (redeems seem)   (staring _____)

7. (shut hut)   (grub _____)   (bran ran)

8. (bush bus)   (team _____)   (song son)

9. (rotten not)   (logged _____)   (mitten nit)

Make a word from two other words

In these questions, the word in the middle of the second group is made in the
same way as the word in the middle of the first group.
Find the word that is missing in the second group and write it on the line.

10. (weed [tore] root)   (pies [_____] tall)

11. (white [with] trawl)   (height [_____] crane)

12. (wand [dawn] dear)   (bust [_____] tent)

13. (bangs [bond] bound)   (stale [_____] lines)

14. (flower [slow] houses)   (thanks [_____] hostels)

15. (windows [chins] coaches)   (barrage [_____] whisper)

16. (weep [pray] tray)   (door [_____] sing)

17. (table [grab] green)   (misty [_____] there)

18. (fancy [funny] haiku)   (burly [_____] prime)

Synonyms

Synonyms are words with similar meanings. Synonym questions test your understanding of word meaning and word type.

Words of a similar meaning

For example: Underline the **two** words, **one** from each group, that are most similar in meaning.

(hot cool heat)   (oven ice cold)

First, **scan** the words. The answer may be obvious. If it is not, compare each word in the first set to each word in the second set. Work through the words in turn.

- Are **hot** and **oven** similar in meaning? No.
- Are **hot** and **ice** similar in meaning? No.
- Are **hot** and **cold** similar in meaning? No.
- Are **cool** and **oven** similar in meaning? No.
- Are **cool** and **ice** similar in meaning? Yes.
- Are **cool** and **cold** similar in meaning? Yes. They are more similar in meaning than **cool** and **ice**.

Answer: (hot <u>cool</u> heat)   (oven ice <u>cold</u>)

 Underline the **two** words, **one** from each group, that are most similar in meaning.

  1. (almost always never)   (sometimes nearly now)

  2. (repeat reply redo)   (undo answer refuse)

  3. (sturdy detail fragile)   (delicate broken grand)

  4. (essential essence easy)   (hard important difficult)

  5. (diminish dessert disaster)   (leave reduce increase)

  6. (strong weak week)   (small frail month)

Hint   If you are unsure, put each word into a sentence. For example, 'I **almost** won the race.' / 'I **nearly** won the race.' If the meaning stays the same, your choice is correct.

Synonyms

Words of a similar type or meaning

Some questions may contain words of a similar type rather than words that are similar in meaning.

For example: Find and underline the **two** words that are of a similar type or meaning.

apple   mouse   pigeon   pear   green

Compare each word in turn with each of the other words. Think about the meaning. Decide whether the two words have any **connections**.

- Is **apple** similar to **mouse**? No.

- Is **apple** similar to **pigeon**? No.

- Is **apple** similar to **pear**? Yes – they are both types of fruit. The two words are not similar in meaning, but they are of a similar type.

When you think you have found the answer, continue checking the other words. There might be a pair that is more closely connected.

Answer: <u>apple</u>   mouse   pigeon   <u>pear</u>   green

Hint These questions are laid out differently from the **synonym** questions on page 23. Here, you compare each word in turn with **all** the other words given, not just with those in a second group. Watch out for different question types and read the question carefully.

Find and underline the **two** words in each line that are of a similar type or meaning.

1. ask   talk   reply   annoy   question

2. blame   defeat   assure   beat   lose

3. hound   feline   artistic   artful   crafty

4. destiny   detour   aloud   fate   fete

5. class   firm   soft   busy   engaged

6. intent   impolite   distress   rude   polite

7. bicycle   runway   station   bus   wing

8. lamp   kitchen   shed   carpet   bedroom

Antonyms

Antonyms are words that are opposite in meaning. Antonym questions test your understanding of word meanings. They are presented in different ways.

Choosing one word from each of two groups

For example: Underline the **two** words, **one** from each group, that are most opposite in meaning.

(under enter over)   (around exit below)

Scan the words. The answer may be obvious. If it is not, compare each word in the first set to each word in the second set, in turn:

- Are **under** and **around** opposites? No.
- Are **under** and **exit** opposites? No.
- Are **under** and **below** opposites? No.
- Are **enter** and **around** opposites? No.
- Are **enter** and **exit** opposites? Yes.

Answer: (under <u>enter</u> over)   (around <u>exit</u> below)

> **!** These questions look like **synonym** questions. Read them carefully. Look for words that are **opposite** in meaning.

Underline the **two** words, **one** from each group, that are most opposite in meaning.

1. (begin after stop)   (lend land end)

2. (danger despair desperate)   (risk hope fear)

3. (mean dark cold)   (dim dreary kind)

4. (find full fast)   (empty quick found)

5. (healthy include inside)   (hungry interior exclude)

6. (movie genuine genius)   (real fake film)

7. (perfect pendant new)   (brand antique perform)

8. (accept letter gift)   (receive thank reject)

> **Hint** To check your answer, put each word in a sentence. For example, 'I **always** eat my greens.' / 'I **never** eat my greens.' If swapping the words gives the sentence the opposite meaning, your answer is probably right.

Choosing one pair of words from three given

Example: Underline the **pair** of words that are most opposite in meaning.

(above, over) (poppy, daffodil) (large, small)

Answer:
(above, over) (poppy, daffodil) (<u>large, small</u>)

Examine each pair of words. Think about their meaning:

- **Above** and **over** have similar meanings. Are they opposites? No.
- **Poppy** and **daffodil** are both types of flower. Are they opposites? No.
- **Large** and **small** are both describing words. Are they opposites? Yes.

Underline the **pair** of words that are most opposite in meaning.

1. (better, superior) (orange, banana) (mad, sane)

2. (maximum, minimum) (loud, noisy) (father, uncle)

3. (beautiful, pretty) (powerful, feeble) (victory, vanity)

4. (happy, cheerful) (house, garden) (demand, supply)

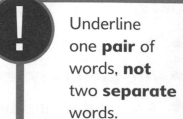

! Underline one **pair** of words, **not** two **separate** words.

Hint If you are unsure of some word meanings, rule out the answers you know are wrong, then guess.

Choosing one word that is opposite to a single word given

Example: Underline the **one** word **inside** the brackets that is most **opposite** in meaning to the word **before** the brackets.

cheap (noisy, happy, expensive, bargain, shopping)

Answer:
cheap (noisy, happy, <u>expensive</u>, bargain, shopping)

Think about the meaning of the word outside the brackets. Compare it in turn to each word inside the brackets. Think about the different meanings:

- Are **cheap** and **noisy** opposites? No.
- Are **cheap** and **happy** opposites? No.
- Are **cheap** and **expensive** opposites? Yes.

Find and underline the **one** word **inside** the brackets that is most **opposite** in meaning to the word **before** the brackets.

5. knowledge (wisdom, lazy, legal, question, ignorance)

6. hinder (hamper, annoy, help, hind, honest)

7. encourage (enthusiastic, bored, praise, discourage, disagree)

Analogies

An **analogy** is a comparison. In verbal reasoning analogy questions, you look for ways in which two words relate to one another. Then you find another two words that relate to each other in a similar way.

For example: Cow is to (field, fish, calf) as **pig** is to (snout, piglet, animal).

The connection must be the same for both halves of the sentence.

- First, **scan** the words. The correct answer may be obvious. If it is not, read the options carefully and follow these steps.

- Compare the first word (**cow**) to each of the choices in turn. Do the words relate to each other? If so, in what way?
  - ♦ **cow – field**: are they connected? Yes: a **cow** lives in a **field**. Look at the words in the second set. Is there a word relating to **pig** in the same way? No: move on to the next word.
  - ♦ **cow – fish**: are they connected? No: move on to the next word.
  - ♦ **cow – calf**: are they connected? Yes: a **calf** is a **baby cow**. Look to see if there is a word that relates to **pig** in the same way.

- Each time you look at the second set of words, you look for a connection that is similar to one of the connections you have found in the first set.
  - ♦ **pig – snout**: are they connected? Yes, but not in the same way as **cow** and **field** or **cow** and **calf**.
  - ♦ **pig – piglet**: are they connected? Yes: a **piglet** is a **baby pig**. The words are connected in the same way as **cow** and **calf**.

> **!** Once you think you have found the answer, read the sentence carefully. Check that the same comparison is made in both halves. Then underline the two words.

Answer: Cow is to (field, fish, <u>**calf**</u>) as **pig** is to (snout, <u>**piglet**</u>, animal).

 Underline the **two** words, **one** from each group, that complete the sentence in the best way.

1. Fish is to (walk, run, swim) as bird is to (trot, fly, jump).

2. Grass is to (long, green, mow) as sand is to (warm, beach, yellow).

3. Uncle is to (old, son, aunt) as sister is to (mother, girl, brother).

4. Eleven is to (twelve, number, two) as four is to (seven, for, five).

5. Teacher is to (bank, park, school) as mechanic is to (car, garage, tip).

There are four types of **analogy** questions: similar meanings, opposites, real-life **connections** and spelling connections. For examples of similar meanings questions, see page 27. Examples of the other question types are given below and on page 29.

Opposites

For example:
Contest is to (game, rugby, agree) as **light** is to (lamp, heavy, warm).

- **Scan** the words. The answer may be obvious.

- Compare the first word (**contest**) to **game**, **rugby** and **agree**.
  - ◆ **contest – game** and **contest – rugby** make you think of the meaning 'competition'.
  - ◆ **contest – agree** reminds you that **contest** also means 'disagree'.

- Now look at the second set of words.
  - ◆ **light – lamp** makes you think of the meaning 'brightness'.
  - ◆ **light – heavy** reminds you that **light** also means 'not heavy'.

- An **opposites** connection works in both parts of the sentence. **Contest** is the opposite of **agree**. **Light** is the opposite of **heavy**.

- Check again that the same comparison is made in both halves of the sentence.

Answer: Contest is to (game, rugby, <u>agree</u>) as **light** is to (lamp, <u>heavy</u>, warm).

Hint   Look out for words that have more than one meaning.

 Underline the **two** words, **one** from each group, that complete the sentence in the best way.

1. Left is to (leave, right, wrong) as horizontal is to (sun, across, vertical).

2. Attack is to (fight, win, defend) as expand is to (extinct, contract, explain).

3. Fresh is to (stale, edible, air) as humble is to (old, pie, proud).

4. Rush is to (dawdle, jog, skip) as adequate is to (inadequate, less, quad).

5. Clear is to (wash, cloudy, simple) as late is to (eight, cup, early).

Analogies

Real-life connections

This is the most common connection. It covers many topics.

For example:
Ship is to (port, boat, sea) as lorry is to (petrol, driver, road).

Scan the words. If the answer is not obvious, work through the options.

- The word **ship** has connections with **port**, **boat** and **sea**.
- Only **one** of these connections is the same in both halves.
- A **ship** travels on the **sea**. A **lorry** travels on the **road**.

Answer: Ship is to (port, boat, <u>sea</u>) as lorry is to (petrol, driver, <u>road</u>).

Spelling connections

These connections focus on letters, not meaning. There are three question types. The words in each pair:

- are **homophones**

  For example: Sea is to (water, <u>see</u>, boat) as sent is to (parcel, spent, <u>scent</u>).

- are made by adding or removing a letter

  For example: Port is to (<u>pot</u>, ferry, wine) as bear is to (beer, <u>bar</u>, spider).

- have the same letters but in a different **order**

  For example: Draw is to (well, drawer, <u>ward</u>) as rate is to (race, <u>tear</u>, opinion).

Hint Remember the analogy types: similar meanings, opposites, real-life connections, spelling connections. Scan for an answer. Then work through each possibility.

Underline the **two** words, **one** from each group, that complete the sentence in the best way.

1. Main is to (horse, mane, least) as sight is to (picture, taste, site).

2. Gardener is to (plants, grow, spade) as painter is to (artist, brush, colour).

3. Stag is to (deer, doe, antlers) as bull is to (horns, calf, field).

4. Taps is to (tops, money, spat) as dab is to (dot, bad, dip).

5. Tree is to (trunk, twigs, roots) as building is to (flat, foundations, home).

Odd one out

Odd ones out questions test your understanding of word meaning. You are given five words. You have to find the **two** words that do not go with the other three.

For example: Underline the **two** words that are different from the other three.

giraffe   horse   octopus   cow   eel

First, find the three words that **go together**.
Look at each word in turn. Compare it to each of the others. Find what the words have **in common**.

- Are **giraffe** and **horse** connected? Yes – both animals with four legs and both mammals.
- Are **giraffe** and **octopus** connected? No.
- Are **giraffe** and **cow** connected? Yes – both animals with four legs and both mammals.
- Are **giraffe** and **eel** connected? No.

Giraffe, **horse** and **cow** are the three that go together.

The two words that are different are **octopus** and **eel**.

Answer: giraffe   horse   <u>octopus</u>   cow   <u>eel</u>

Find and underline the **two** words in each group that are different from the other three.

1. rose   mosquito   daffodil   cricket   tulip

2. mechanic   accountant   organ   solicitor   guitar

3. delight   dismay   joy   despair   misery

4. glider   helicopter   airship   yacht   canoe

5. mole   owl   badger   fox   kestrel

6. apple   lettuce   mango   salad   kiwi

 Hint   The odd ones out may or may not go with each other.

Word connections

These questions test your knowledge of words with more than one meaning.

For example: Here are two pairs of words. Choose from the five possible answers the **one** word that goes equally well with **both** the word pairs. Underline the word.

cost good fine joyful price (fee, penalty) (well, happy)

Read the words in brackets. Think about the meanings and how they are connected. Look at each of the five words in turn. Look for a **connection** with the words in brackets:

- Is **cost** connected with **fee, penalty**? Yes – to do with paying money.
- Is **cost** connected with **well, happy**? No.
- Is **good** connected with **fee, penalty**? No.
- Is **fine** connected with **fee, penalty**? Yes – to do with paying money.
- Is **fine** connected with **well, happy**? Yes – to do with feeling good.

Answer: cost good <u>fine</u> joyful price

In the questions below, there are two pairs of words. Choose from the five possible answers the **one** word that goes equally well with both pairs. Underline the word.

1. boat upset row swim disagree (paddle, propel) (fight, argue)

2. break wail sob tear spoil (rip, cut) (cry, weep)

3. bruise splint spiral revolve wound (injury, hurt) (turned, twisted)

4. doctor ill invalid used nurse (patient, injured) (defunct, obsolete)

5. door distant close conceal hide (shut, cover) (near, almost)

6. soil sow boar grow animal (plant, cultivate) (pig, hog)

Hint   Think of different pronunciations and meanings of the words. For example, **bow** can mean 'a knot with two loops' or 'to bend forward from the waist'. The meaning depends on the pronunciation.

Now test your skills with these practice pages. If you get stuck, go back to pages 23 to 31 for some reminders.

Synonyms

Underline the **two** words, **one** from each group, that are most similar in meaning.

1. (bargain question baffle)   (confuse price answer)

2. (thankful bold afraid)   (bald fearless praise)

3. (sweet sour batter)   (bitter lemon arrive)

4. (free compliment complex)   (flatter argue ignore)

5. (offer beginner began)   (novice cause ending)

Antonyms

Underline the **two** words, **one** from each group, that are most opposite in meaning.

6. (new ancient ancestor)   (modern moderate moreover)

7. (artificial arrange entrance)   (fake natural unkind)

8. (knife bent blunt)   (crooked spoon sharp)

9. (cold vague alert)   (vanish clear cloudy)

10. (slack slip victory)   (win tight victor)

Analogies

Underline the **two** words, **one** from each group, that complete the sentence in the best way.

11. Over is to (down, under, out) as enter is to (entrance, into, exit).

12. Racquet is to (noise, badminton, cricket) as stick is to (tree, hockey, glue).

13. Ball is to (cry, bawl, bowl) as seam is to (seal, dress, seem).

14. Fashion is to (clothes, trend, model) as bet is to (wager, bat, win).

15. Clarinet is to (music, wind, play) as drum is to (percussion, sticks, loud).

16. Apple is to (fruit, red, pip) as plum is to (vegetable, juicy, stone).

17. Leap is to (pale, jump, high) as rear is to (rare, rhyme, steer).

Odd ones out

Underline the **two** words in each group that are different from the other three.

1. birch oak acorn flower willow

2. school college church university temple

3. anger fear rage fury delight

4. crib sleep bed cot dream

5. youth doctor infant nurse child

6. increase reduce diminish inflate lessen

7. trout salmon seal cod dolphin

8. mother brother uncle sister wife

9. sadness joy mourning jubilation misery

Word connections

In the questions below, there are two pairs of words. Choose from the five possible answers the **one** word that goes equally well with both pairs. Underline the word.

10. money church change repair jottings (coins, notes) (alter, amend)

11. draft twist hurricane wind spin (gale, breeze) (turn, rotate)

12. subject learn hurt expert plan (topic, lesson) (inflict, expose)

13. toilet waste dress sewer haberdasher (drain, effluent) (seamstress, tailor)

14. sand beach sign hand wave (sea, water) (gesture, signal)

15. galaxy planet star moon hero (sun, comet) (famous, idol)

16. holdall cause support case pouch (argument, defence) (bag, cover)

17. leave land grass stay enter (alight, arrive) (ground, earth)

18. weaker number integer pain seven (figure, numeral) (duller, soothed)

Missing letter

In these questions, you are given a pair of words. A letter is missing from the end of the first word and the beginning of the second word. You have to find the **one** missing letter that completes both words.

For example: Find the letter that will end the first word and start the second.

gra (?) agic

- Look at the incomplete words. Say them in your head. The answer may come to you.

- If it does not, go through the alphabet. Try each letter in turn. Add it to the end of the first word.

  gra (a) = graa   Is this a word? No – move on to the next letter.

- Once you have found a letter that spells a word, try the same letter at the beginning of the second word.

  gra (b) = grab   Is this a word? Yes – try it with the second word.

  (b) agic = bagic   Is this a word? No.

- Work through the alphabet to find another letter that completes the first word. Try it with the second word. Repeat until you find a letter that completes both words.

  gra (m) = gram   Is this a word? Yes – try it with the second word.

  (m) agic = magic   Is this a word? Yes.

Answer: gra (m) agic

- If you have no luck with the first word, work with the second word instead.

> **!** In multiple choice tests you are given a choice of five letters. Try each letter in turn, as above.

Find the letter that will end the first word and start the second word. Write it on the line.

1. spin (e) yes
2. strea (m) eat
3. gree (n) omb
4. sou (p) iglet
5. tow (n) eck
6. sof (a) pple

Sometimes you are given two pairs of words, both with the same letter missing.

For example: Find the **one** missing letter that will complete both pairs of words. It will end the words before the brackets and start the words after the brackets.

man (?) olk   buo (?) awn

The technique is the same as for one pair of words. However, once you have found a letter to complete the first pair you must try the same letter with the second pair too.

- **man (e) = mane**   Is this a word? Yes – try it with the second word.
- **(e) olk = eolk**   Is this a word? No – try a different letter with the first word.
- **man (y) = many**   Is this a word? Yes – try it with the second word.
- **(y) olk = yolk**   Is this a word? Yes – try it with the third word.
- **buo (y) = buoy**   Is this a word? Yes – try it with the fourth word.
- **(y) awn = yawn**   Is this a word? Yes.

Answer: man (y) olk   buo (y) awn

Find the **one** missing letter that will complete both pairs of words.

1. wal (k) ing   mil (k) ite
2. cla (y) ine   lea (y) ound
3. wav (e) at   tim (e) arth
4. stin (g) nat   dra (g) lare
5. trai (n) ought   gri (n) ear
6. mil (t) ake   stea (t) ive
7. shove (l) ost   towe (l) ower
8. mont (h) igh   yout (h) and

Hint   Say the different sounds that the letters can make. For example, vowel sounds can be long or short and some letters combine to make a new sound.

Move a letter

In these questions, you are given two words. You take a letter from the first word so that it leaves a correctly spelt word. You then put the same letter into the second word to make another word. The **order** of the letters cannot be changed.

For example: Move **one** letter from the first word to the second word to make **two** new words.

first   tack

- Look at the first word. Cover each letter in turn. Do the remaining letters make a real word?

    f̸irst = irst   Is this a real word? No.

    fi̸rst = frst   Is this a real word? No.

    fir̸st = fist   Is this a real word? Yes.

- Once you have made a real word, put the same letter in front of the first letter of the second word. Try it in every position in turn.

    rtack   Is this a real word? No.

    track   Is this a real word? Yes.

Answer: r moves, to make **<u>fist</u>** and **<u>track</u>**

Move **one** letter from the first word to the second word to make **two** new words.

   1. spray   eat   : __ moves, to make _____ and _____

   2. brought   down   : __ moves, to make _____ and _____

   3. clamp   hill   : __ moves, to make _____ and _____

   4. trust   burn   : __ moves, to make _____ and _____

   5. brand   head   : __ moves, to make _____ and _____

   6. grain   bean   : __ moves, to make _____ and _____

Hint If you find it difficult to imagine the new words, write them down. Then you will find them easier to check.

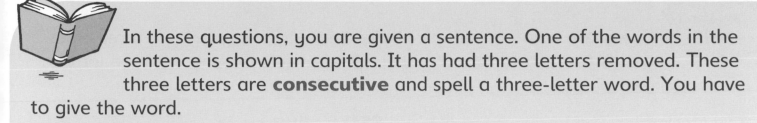

Missing three letters

In these questions, you are given a sentence. One of the words in the sentence is shown in capitals. It has had three letters removed. These three letters are **consecutive** and spell a three-letter word. You have to give the word.

For example: It was an exciting football **CH**.

- Read the sentence carefully. The answer may come to you.

- If it does not, read the sentence again. Think of a word that would make sense. Does it contain the letters given?

  It was an exciting football ... **GAME**? No – doesn't contain **C** and **H**. **MATCH**? Yes – contains **C** and **H**.

- Write out the whole word, crossing out the letters given.

  MAT~~CH~~   The missing three letters spell **MAT**.

Answer: MAT

The word or letter in capitals has had three letters next to each other taken out. These three letters make one correctly spelt word without changing the order. Write the word.

1. Would you like this cake or **T** one? _____

2. I went to **VI** my grandmother in hospital. _____

3. I **SPED** over on the ice. _____

4. My little sister **WS** a doll for her birthday. _____

5. **W** do you get your exam results? _____

6. The grey wolf **HED** at the moon. _____

7. My **GDMA** needs to wear her glasses for reading. _____

8. I went to the shop and **ST** all my pocket money. _____

9. For dinner, we had chicken and brown **R**. _____

10. She walked carefully down the steep **SE**. _____

 Hint   Before you write the answer, write the longer word in full to make sure the spelling looks right.

If you are doing a multiple choice test, you are given five three-letter words to choose from. You try each possible answer with the letters given.

For example: The boy jumped out and **SED** his little sister.

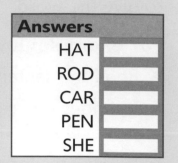

Answers	
HAT	
ROD	
CAR	
PEN	
SHE	

- Read the sentence. Look at the answers given. The answer may come to you.

- If it does not, look at the word with the missing letters. Decide where the letters may have been taken from, then try them out.

  ED often comes at the end of a word. So the missing letters are either at the beginning or after the **S**. First, try each answer at the **start** of the word.

  HAT**SED** ROD**SED** CAR**SED** PEN**SED** SHE**SED** None of these are real words.

  Next, try each answer **after** the **S**.

  S**HAT**ED S**ROD**ED S**CAR**ED Answer option **C (CAR)** makes **SCARED**. This is a real word.

- Check that your chosen word makes sense in the sentence.

  The boy jumped out and **SCARED** his little sister.

Answer: C

The word in capitals has had three letters next to each other taken out. These three letters make one correctly spelt word without changing the **order**. Find the word. Mark it with a **horizontal** line like this ▬ in the answer box.

1. My dad went into **HOSAL** for an operation.

2. The old lady was **ALED** by the tragic news.

3. You need to press the 'on' **SCH** to make it work.

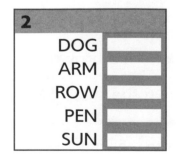

1	
PUT	
MOP	
ARE	
LEG	
PIT	

2	
DOG	
ARM	
ROW	
PEN	
SUN	

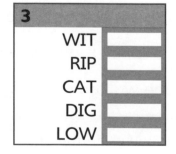

3	
WIT	
RIP	
CAT	
DIG	
LOW	

Spot the word

In these questions, you are given a sentence. There is a four-letter word hidden at the end of one word and the beginning of the next. You have to find the hidden word.

For example: I wonder how she did in her maths test.

- Read the sentence carefully. The answer may be obvious.

- If it is not, go through the sentence. Look at the end of each word and the beginning of the next. It may help to cover the other letters so that you only see four letters at once. Carry on until you spot a four-letter word.

 The word must be split across two words. A word hidden inside another word does not count.

I wonder how she did in her maths test.   Is **iwon** a word? No.

I won**der h**ow she did in her maths test.   Is **dehr** a word? No.

I wond**er ho**w she did in her maths test.   Is **erho** a word? No.

I wonde**r how** she did in her maths test.   Is **rhow** a word? No.

I wonder **how s**he did in her maths test.   Is **hows** a word? No.

I wonder h**ow sh**e did in her maths test.   Is **owsh** a word? No.

I wonder ho**w she** did in her maths test.   Is **wshe** a word? No.

I wonder how **she d**id in her maths test.   Is **shed** a word? Yes.

Answer: <u>shed</u>

Remember that in all questions of this type you are looking for a four-letter word. There are only three possible letter combinations between every two **adjacent** words:

- **three** letters in the first word and **one** letter in the **second**.

- **two** letters in the first word and **two** letters in the **second**.

- **one** letter in the first word and **three** letters in the **second**.

Spot the word

Find the hidden four-letter word in each sentence below. Underline the word and write it on the line.

! The hidden word may span three words.
For example: She wa<u>s a me</u>dal winner at the Olympics. (same)

1. Have you seen them eat their meal yet? _____

2. My uncle had his own aeroplane. _____

3. You need a warm oven for baking bread. _____

4. The dreadful storm was a weather disaster. _____

5. I like to jog one mile each day. _____

6. Nervously, the competitors entered the ring. _____

7. Sally scored the most points in the test. _____

8. He was the first opponent to cross the line. _____

9. There was a sudden thunder crash. _____

10. New employees bring new ideas. _____

11. Some children think teachers know everything. _____

12. The views alter depending on the light. _____

13. Some seeds never germinate but these always do. _____

14. Felt tips for sale – five in a packet! _____

15. Reaching the peak would be a tough climb. _____

16. The aging lady climbed out of the carriage. _____

17. I am a keen swimmer but I prefer tennis. _____

18. Have a chocolate if you'd like one! _____

19. My T-shirt had a long rip down the back. _____

20. All members of the club train daily. _____

Join two words to make one

In these questions, you are given two groups of words. You have to find the **two** words (**one** from each group) that together make **one** new word. The word from the first group comes first.

For example: (day night moon)   (sleep over mare)

● Try each word in the first group with each word in the second until you find a word.

day + **sleep** = **daysleep**   Is this a real word? No.

day + **over** = **dayover**   Is this a real word? No.

day + **mare** = **daymare**   Is this a real word? No.

night + **sleep** = **nightsleep**   Is this a real word? No.

night + **over** = **nightover**   Is this a real word? No.

night + **mare** = **nightmare**   Is this a real word? Yes.

● Write the word down. Does it look right?

Answer: <u>nightmare</u>

  The word may sound right but make sure that it is spelt right too.

 Underline the **two** words, **one** from each group, that together make **one** new word. The word from the first group comes first.

1. (can key car)   (band board bored)

2. (puff poor peer)   (on in out)

3. (by but be)   (hind hound hand)

4. (end and under)   (less loss lass)

5. (about over even)   (near give take)

6. (paint path pass)   (port part pant)

Hint   If you cannot find the new word, write down all the possible combinations. The correct one is then easier to spot.

Join two words to make one

The sound of two words may change when they are put together.

For example:

car + rot = carrot   The long **ar** sound in **car** changes to a short **a** sound when put together with **rot**.

prim + ate = primate   The short **i** sound changes to a long sound when the words are combined.

tea + ring = tearing   The long **ee** sound in **tea** changes to an **air** sound when joined with **ring**.

As you read the words, experiment with the letter sounds:

- Change the vowel sound from long to short or short to long.

- Think about the letter blends (for example, **th**, **oo**, **ea**). If one word ends in **t** and another begins with **h** there is a **th** sound in the middle of the new word. For example, **slit + her = slither**. The **t** and **h** combine to make **th**.

Underline the **two** words, **one** from each group, that together make **one** new word. The word from the first group comes first.

  1. (tar bar car)　(grin gain ten)

  2. (post most pine)　(age and or)

  3. (is us as)　(queen king prince)

  4. (yes not all)　(is in ice)

  5. (up so it)　(lid led lad)

  6. (he him her)　(row air art)

  7. (miss to let)　(ward take end)

  8. (sign train grow)　(ape post aim)

  9. (tear bar out)　(round key row)

10. (and out so)　(at on off)

Hint　Look out for common word endings in the second group, such as **ing**, **er**, **en**, **le**, **y**. Think about how they sound at the end of a word.

Join two words to make one

You may be asked to find **one** word that can go in front of a group of words to make a new set of words. A word that goes in front is called a **prefix**.

For example: Find a word that can be put in front of each word to make four new words.

coat   bow   storm   proof

- Think of as many words as you can that end with the first word (in this example, words ending with **coat** include **overcoat**, **turncoat**, **raincoat**).
- Try out each prefix (in this example, **over**, **turn**, **rain**) with the other words given, working from left to right.

over + **coat** = **overcoat**

over + **bow** = **overbow**   Is this a real word? No

turn + **coat** = **turncoat**

turn + **bow** = **turnbow**   Is this a real word? No

rain + **coat** = **raincoat**

rain + **bow** = **rainbow**   Is this a real word? Yes

rain + **storm** = **rainstorm**   Is this a real word? Yes

rain + **proof** = **rainproof**   Is this a real word? Yes

Answer: <u>rain</u>

Find **one** word that can be put in front of each of these words to make four new words.

1. time   light   dream   break _____

2. fall   front   bed   wheel _____

3. shell   shore   weed   sick _____

4. set   shine   down   tan _____

5. pack   ward   hand   ground _____

6. craft   port   brush   ship _____

Spelling practice page 1

Now test your skills with these practice pages.
If you get stuck, go back to pages 34 to 43 for some reminders.

Missing letter

Find the **one** missing letter that completes both pairs of words.

1. arm (_y_) our   pla (_y_) acht
2. clo (_g_) oal   han (_g_) ive
3. mat (_e_) asy   win (_e_) ven
4. blin (_k_) nit   trac (_k_) ing
5. floo (_d_) rive   roun (_d_) amp
6. fla (_p_) ansy   stee (_p_) iano
7. meta (_l_) iver   grow (_l_) oose
8. dra (_w_) indy   fla (_w_) eary

Move a letter

Move **one** letter from the first word to the second word to make **two** new words. Write the new words.

9. dream   wed   _____   _____

10. shave   barn   _____   _____

11. cream   trip   _____   _____

12. naive   led   _____   _____

13. pleat   mode   _____   _____

14. could   bond   _____   _____

15. lived   alley   _____   _____

16. thorn   boot   _torn_   _booth_

Spelling practice page 2

Missing three letters

In each of the following sentences, the word in bold has three letters missing. Those three letters spell a word. Write the three-letter word.

1. Can you **AGE** to eat any more? _____

2. The playground had a swing and a **SE**. _____

3. I had to write a long **ES** for my coursework. _____

4. The priest lit a **DLE** for peace. _____

5. Use the jug for **PING** water. _____

6. The **SNING** top whirled round and round. _____

7. We decorated the Christmas tree with lights and **SEL**. _____

Spot the word

Find the hidden four-letter word in each sentence below. Underline the word and write it on the line.

8. It's time to gather the crops. _____

9. She smiled her brightest smile. _____

10. Sweep up the leaves and rubbish, please. _____

11. Laugh and smile every day! _____

12. He arrived late and Mum was cross. _____

13. It's important not to waste a minute! _____

Join two words to make one

Underline the **two** words, **one** from each group, that together make **one** word. The word from the first group comes first.

14. (up count sing)   (out down in)

15. (door roof window)   (letter out man)

16. (round under through)   (above below about)

17. (head neck fear)   (loss list lace)

18. (about over even)   (near give take)

19. (is be as)   (an up off)

Number sequences

In these questions, you are given a **series** of numbers. You look for a pattern and find the next number.

For example: 2   5   8   11   14   (?)

- Work out the gap between each number. Write it above.

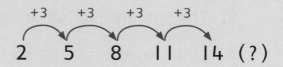

- Continue the pattern to find the answer.   14 + 3 = 17

Answer: <u>17</u>

Addition, subtraction, repetition

There are different pattern types to look out for. Here are the first few, with examples.

- Adding or subtracting the same number

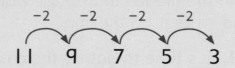

- Adding or subtracting an increasing amount

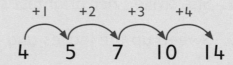

- Adding or subtracting a decreasing amount

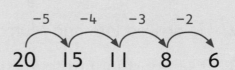

- Repeating patterns

or

Find the next number in the **sequence** and write it on the line.

1. 8   11   14   17   20 (_____)   **4.** 18   15   12   9   6 (_____)

2. 25   20   16   13   11 (_____)   **5.** 28   26   23   22   20   17 (_____)

3. 12   14   17   19   22 (_____)   **6.** 16   22   27   31   34 (_____)

Number sequences

Multiplying, dividing

Here are some more patterns, with examples:

- multiply or divide by the same number

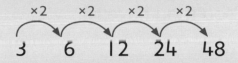

$$3 \quad 6 \quad 12 \quad 24 \quad 48$$

- multiply or divide by an increasing number

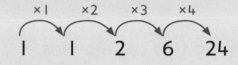

$$1 \quad 1 \quad 2 \quad 6 \quad 24$$

- multiply or divide by a decreasing number

$$120 \quad 30 \quad 10 \quad 5 \quad 5$$

> **Hint** Learn your times tables and the division facts that go with them. For example, if $2 \times 4 = 8$, then $4 \times 2 = 8$, $8 \div 4 = 2$ and $8 \div 2 = 4$.

 Find the next number in the sequence and write it on the line.

1. 2 4 8 16 (_____)

2. 160 80 40 20 (_____)

3. 1 3 9 27 (_____)

4. 400 200 100 50 (_____)

5. 5 25 100 300 (_____)

6. 96 48 24 12 (_____)

7. 10 50 200 600 (_____)

8. 1800 300 60 15 (_____)

9. 7 21 63 189 (_____)

10. 1200 120 12 1.2 (_____)

> **Hint** Learn key number facts, such as pairs of numbers that make 10 and 20, halves and doubles, addition and subtraction facts up to 20.

Hidden patterns

Sometimes, the **sequences** involve patterns that are harder to spot.

You may have to:

- add the previous two numbers

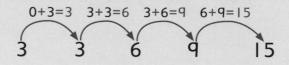

- do two calculations ('double **operations**')

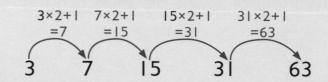

- jump to the next number but one (**leapfrogging**, as described on page 5). Jump over the last number to get to the answer.

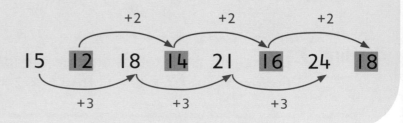

Find the next number in the **sequence** and write it on the line.

1. 3 2 5 4 7 6 (_____)

2. 30 4 25 8 20 16 (_____)

3. 1 2 3 5 8 (_____)

4. 5 10 15 25 40 (_____)

5. 2 5 11 23 47 (_____)

6. 120 80 60 40 30 20 (_____)

7. 12 12 24 36 60 96 (_____)

8. 4 18 46 102 214 (_____)

9. 1 7 3 14 5 21 7 28 (_____)

10. 2 5 4 10 6 15 (_____)

Number sequences

Squared and cubed numbers

Some sequences contain **squared** or **cubed** numbers.

A squared number is a number multiplied by itself.

For example: $2 \times 2 = 4$
$3 \times 3 = 9$
$4 \times 4 = 16$

4, 9 and **16** are all squared numbers (or 'squares').
Squared numbers are sometimes written like this: $2^2 = 4$, $3^2 = 9$.

A squared numbers sequence might look like this
4 9 16 25 36 or like this 81 64 49 36 25.

A cubed number is a number multiplied by itself **twice**.

For example: $2 \times 2 \times 2 = 8$
$3 \times 3 \times 3 = 27$

8 and **27** are both cubed numbers (or 'cubes').
Cubed numbers are sometimes written like this: $2^3 = 8$, $3^3 = 27$.

A cubed numbers sequence might look like this: 27 64 125 216.

Find the next number in the sequence and write it on the line.

1. 27 64 125 216 (_____)

2. 36 49 64 81 (_____)

3. 9 16 25 36 (_____)

4. 216 125 64 27 (_____)

Missing from the middle

Sometimes the missing numbers are in the middle of the sequence.
You then look at the **adjacent** numbers in order to spot the pattern.

For example:

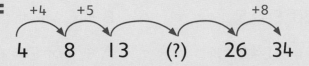

+4 +5   +8
4   8   13   (?)   26   34

The jumps increase by one each time. $13 + 6 = 19$. The sequence continues with $19 + 7 = 26$.

Answer: 19

Find the missing number in the sequence and write it on the line.

5. 2 4 6 10 (_____) 26

6. 1 3 7 (_____) 31 63

7. 40 8 (_____) 16 20 24 10

8. (_____) 6 11 17 28 45

Letters for numbers

In these questions you are given a sum using letters instead of numbers. Using information given, you work out the answer to the sum. You write your answer as a letter.

For example: A=4, B=5, C=6, D=3, E=9.

What is the answer to this sum, written as a letter?

A + B − C = (?)

- First, write the numbers represented by the letters underneath each letter in the sum.
  A + B − C =
  4 + 5 − 6 =

- Then **calculate** the answer one step at a time.
  4 + 5 = 9
  and then 9 − 6 = 3

  If it is a tricky sum, write the answer to each step as you go.

- Find the letter that represents your answer.

  *You know from the information given that **D**=3.
  So 3 is represented by the letter **D**.*

Answer: <u>D</u>

- Carefully check the letter that represents your final answer.

Use the information given to answer the sum. Write your answer as a letter.

1. A=6, B=13, C=5, D=3, E=16.   D + B = (___)

2. A=10, B=4, C=8, D=20, E=40.   B × A = (___)

3. A=3, B=13, C=5, D=20, E=15.   B + C − E = (___)

4. A=36, B=6, C=48, D=42, E=8.   A ÷ B × E = (___)

5. A=164, B=168, C=8, D=20, E=160.   C × D + C = (___)

6. A=50, B=12, C=18, D=20, E=40.   D + B + C = (___)

Hint If your answer is not there, check that you have copied the correct numbers under the letters. Then check each step of the calculation.

Missing number

These questions are often called **equations**. An equation is a number sentence where the two amounts on either side of the equals sign (=) have the same total. The aim is to find the missing number (?) so that the number sentence is correct. The amount on both sides of the equals sign must be equal.

For example:

Find the missing number in this equation: 7 + 5 = 20 − (?)

- Calculate the answer to the first half of the equation.
  7 + 5 = 12

- Work out what number you subtract from 20 to make 12.
  20 − (?) = 12

You do this by swapping the two halves of the equation.

To find the answer, either count up from 12 to 20 or subtract 12 from 20.

Answer: <u>8</u>

Hint Read the question carefully. Do the correct **operation**. Calculate each step and write your answers as you go.

Find the missing number in these equations and write it on the line.

1. 6 + 5 = 13 − (___)

2. 14 − 7 = 2 + (___)

3. 6 × 3 = 25 − (___)

4. 25 ÷ 5 = 1 + (___)

5. 30 − 16 = 7 × (___)

6. 23 + 41 = 8 × (___)

7. 18 ÷ 6 = 12 ÷ (___)

8. 4 × 4 = 2 × (___)

9. 32 − 12 = 20 + (___)

10. 11 + 33 = 11 × (___)

Hint Make sure that you understand the **inverse** operation and how to use it. The inverse of addition is subtraction. The inverse of multiplication is division. (For example, 5 × 6 = 30, 6 × 5 = 30, 30 ÷ 6 = 5, 30 ÷ 5= 6.)

Missing number

The level of difficulty of these questions varies. There may be several steps on each side of the **equation**.

For example:
Find the missing number in this equation: $18 \div 6 + 9 = 3 \times 6 - (?)$

- The technique is as before. **Calculate** each step separately.
  $18 \div 6 = 3$
  $3 + 9 = 12$

  So the first half of the equation equals 12.

- Now, work out the first step in the second part of the equation.
  $3 \times 6 = 18$

- Use your findings to write both halves of the equation again.
  $12 = 18 - (?)$

  Work out what number you subtract from 18 to make 12, or count up from 12 to 18.

Answer: 6

Find the missing number in these equations and write it on the line.

1. $8 + 14 + 12 = 19 + (\underline{\quad})$

2. $14 - 7 = 5 + (\underline{\quad})$

3. $6 \times 3 + 12 = 15 \times (\underline{\quad})$

4. $40 \div 5 - 2 = 28 - 14 - (\underline{\quad})$

5. $240 - 50 - 100 = 67 + (\underline{\quad})$

6. $27 \div 9 \times 100 = 70 \times 3 + (\underline{\quad})$

! Where there are several sums within a question, it is usually (but not always) best to do them in this order:

Brackets (the sum inside the brackets must be answered first, but you can ignore those brackets that show you where to write the answer),

Order (anything to the **power** of something, such as 3^2 or 4^3),

Division,

Multiplication,

Addition,

Subtraction.

Remember the **mnemonic**: **BODMAS**.

Number connections

In number **connections** questions, there are three sets of numbers. In each set, the middle number is made by carrying out an **operation** using the two numbers on the outside. You work out what the operation is. Then you find the missing number. It goes in the middle of the third set.

For example: The number in the square brackets is made using the numbers either side. Work out the missing number and write it on the line.

(4 [12] 3)   (5 [20] 4)   (6 [?] 5)

- Study the first set of numbers. **Identify** the operation. (4 [12] 3)

  4 × 3 = 12. So the operation is multiplication.

- Check this works with the second set of numbers. (5 [20] 4)

  5 × 4 = 20. Again the operation is multiplication.

- Apply the same operation to calculate the answer. (6 [?] 5)

  6 × 5 = 30.

Answer: 30

! The calculation used could be addition, subtraction, multiplication or division.

Work out the missing number and write it on the line.

1. (7 [35] 5)   (5 [20] 4)   (4 [___] 6)

2. (12 [20] 8)   (14 [21] 7)   (11 [___] 9)

3. (23 [20] 3)   (31 [23] 8)   (25 [___] 6)

4. (5 [40] 8)   (4 [12] 3)   (5 [___] 3)

5. (4 [10] 40)   (10 [10] 100)   (9 [___] 36)

6. (6 [24] 4)   (11 [44] 4)   (7 [___] 8)

7. (54 [6] 9)   (48 [8] 6)   (72 [___] 9)

8. (36 [15] 21)   (45 [23] 22)   (65 [___] 24)

These questions may involve two steps or **operations**.

For example: Work out the missing number and write it on the line.

(6 [30] 9) (4 [20] 6) (3 [?] 5)
(a   [c]   b)

Call the number on the left **a**, the one on the right **b** and the one in the middle **c**. In the first set of numbers, **a** is **6**, **b** is **9** and **c** is **30**.

- Study the first set of numbers. **Identify** the most likely first step.
  (6 [30] 9)

  The middle number [**c**] is bigger, so the operation is likely to be multiplication or addition.

- Choose an operation to try out first.
  (6 [30] 9)

  Try addition: 6 + 9 = 15.
  But **c** is 30. How could you get from 15 to 30?
  There are two possibilities for the second step:
  15 + 15 = 30 **or** 15 × 2 = 30.
  These may be shown as **a** + **b** + 15 **or a** + **b** × 2.

- Test your chosen operation with the other set of numbers given:
  (4 [20] 6)

  The first step is **a** + **b**. 4 + 6 = 10.
  Second step, try + 15. But 10 + 15 = 25 not 20.
  So this second step is wrong.
  Try the alternative second step, × 2. 10 × 2 = 20.
  So the two steps are **a** + **b** × 2.

- Finally, apply these two steps (**a** + **b** × 2) to the third set of numbers:
  (3 [?] 5)

  3 + 5 = 8; 8 × 2 = 16.

Answer: <u>16</u>

Hint If you do not find the answer first time, try again with a different first step.

! Learn your multiplication and division facts.

First step

The first step is usually addition, subtraction, multiplication or division using the two numbers on the outside (**a** and **b**). Carry out the first step.

Second step

Work out how you get from that answer to the number in the middle [**c**]. The most common second steps are:

- add one of the numbers on either side (+ **a** or + **b**)

- subtract one of the numbers on either side (− **a** or − **b**)

- add or subtract a random number (+ **z** or − **z**)

- double (× 2) or halve (÷ 2).

Try both steps

Make a note of the two operations, then try them with the second set of numbers. If the same steps work for both sets, use these steps with the third set of numbers to find your answer. If not, try a different first step.

Work out the missing number and write it on the line.

1. (2 [20] 5)   (5 [40] 4)   (4 [__] 6)

2. (6 [10] 3)   (12 [18] 5)   (21 [__] 5)

3. (4 [7] 12)   (3 [11] 15)   (5 [__] 20)

4. (16 [12] 8)   (15 [9] 3)   (14 [__] 10)

5. (12 [14] 3)   (15 [13] 5)   (24 [__] 6)

6. (21 [16] 38) (12 [29] 42) (16 [__] 32)

7. (63 [16] 9)   (56 [15] 7)   (72 [__] 9)

8. (12 [18] 14) (28 [42] 22) (35 [__] 34)

> **Hint** There are sometimes variations to the steps shown above. The steps described here are the most common.

> **!** Try first the operation that looks most likely. Check that the same operations work with both sample sets.

Now test your skills with these practice pages. If you get stuck, go back to pages 46 to 55 for some reminders.

Number sequences

Work out the next number in the **sequence** and write it on the line.

1. 7   14   21   28   35   (___)

2. 6   12   24   48   96   (___)

3. 96   84   72   60   48   (___)

4. 9   16   25   36   49   (___)

5. 8   10   14   20   28   (___)

6. 9   54   18   48   27   42   (___)

7. 4   9   19   39   79   (___)

8. 12   24   36   60   96   (___)

9. 480   240   120   60   (___)

10. 1   8   27   64   (___)

Letters for numbers

In these questions, letters stand for numbers.
Use the information given to answer the sum. Write your answer as a letter.

11.   A=9, B=12, C=15, D=2, E=14   D + B = (___)

12.   A=7, B=4, C=28, D=26, E=21.   B × A = (___)

13.   A=3, B=5, C=7, D=15, E=9.   B + C − E = (___)

14.   A=60, B=12, C=16, D=15, E=3.   A ÷ B × E = (___)

15.   A= 24, B=39, C=42, D=36, E=32.   C + D − B = (___)

16.   A= 65, B=22, C=19, D=24, E=56.   D + B + C = (___)

Missing numbers

Find the missing number that completes the **equation** and write it on the line.

1. 11 + 24 = 40 − (___)

2. 34 − 12 = 15 + (___)

3. 7 × 8 = 20 + (___)

4. 81 ÷ 9 = 3 × (___)

5. 40 − 21 = 17 + (___)

6. 160 ÷ 4 = 7 × 6 − (___)

7. 71 + 20 − 16 = 9 × 4 + (___)

8. 6 × 6 + 4 = 120 ÷ (___)

9. 84 × 2 + 30 = 101 + (___)

10. 74 − 51 + 12 = 38 − (___)

Number connections

The number in the square brackets is made using the numbers either side. Work out the missing number and write it on the line.

11. (3 [24] 8) (6 [54] 9) (7 [___] 6)

12. (16 [28] 12) (19 [32] 13) (15 [___] 18)

13. (45 [30] 15) (54 [32] 22) (73 [___] 26)

14. (72 [8] 9) (48 [6] 8) (110 [___] 10)

15. (13 [16] 29) (52 [11] 63) (46 [___] 84)

16. (16 [20] 8) (27 [30] 9) (40 [___] 5)

17. (12 [35] 3) (6 [65] 11) (4 [___] 7)

18. (24 [51] 37) (43 [67] 34) (21 [___]19)

19. (35 [49] 7) (53 [77] 12) (43 [___] 14)

20. (88 [26] 75) (96 [86] 53) (62 [___] 39)

Days and dates

In problem solving questions you read some information and use this to answer a question.

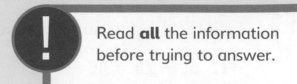

Read **all** the information before trying to answer.

Dates questions involve days of the week or months of the year.

For example: What day was it the day before yesterday if tomorrow is Saturday?

- Write the days of the week, in shortened form.

    M T W Th F̲ (Sa) Su

- Establish what day today is.

    If tomorrow is Saturday, today is Friday, so put your finger on Friday.

- Point to the days as you work through the problem.

    If today is Friday, yesterday must have been Thursday, so the day **before** Thursday would have been Wednesday.

Answer: Wednesday

Hint For questions involving months, write them in shortened form:

Ja Fe Mar (Ap) May Jun Jul Au Se Oc No De

Work out the answer to the question and write it on the line.

1. If tomorrow is Sunday, what day was it yesterday? _Friday_

2. Sam's brother was born in September, three months before his friend, Jack, who was born a month after Stephen.
   In which month was Stephen born? _November_

3. If it is going to be Saturday in three days' time, what day is it today? _Wenesday_

    MTW TH F Sa Son

4. My birthday party took place four days after my birthday, which was on a Wednesday. What day was my party? _Sunday_

5. What month are we in now if last month was two months after Christmas? _March_

6. If next month is May, what month was it the month before last? _Febuary_

Hint Learn key facts: the days in each month, the hours in a day, the weeks in a year.

Some questions involve working out a specific date.

For example: If 5th September is a Monday, what day is 9th November?

- Think which months are between September and November.

  October comes between these two months.

- Jot down the number of days in September and October.

  September: 30 days. October: 31 days.

- Count on from 5th September to find the dates of all the Mondays.

  There are seven days in a week, so by adding sevens you can work out all the Monday dates: 5th, 12th, 19th, 26th September.

- As you reach late September, count on in ones to the end of the month. When you get to 30th September, start again from one.

  Tues 27th Sept, Weds 28th Sept, Thurs 29th Sept, Fri 30th Sept, Sat 1st Oct, Sun 2nd Oct. 3rd October is the first Monday in October.

- Add seven to each date to find the other Mondays in October.

  10th, 17th, 24th, 31st October.

- There are 31 days in October, so count on seven more days to find the first Monday in November.

  The first Monday in November is 7th November.

- 7th November is a Monday.

  9th November is two days after Monday, so it is a Wednesday.

Answer: <u>Wednesday</u>

Work out the answer to the question and write it on the line.

1. If 2nd January is a Saturday, what day is 30th January? _____

2. In a leap year, 1st February falls on a Monday. How many Wednesdays would there be in March? _____

3. If 5th August is a Sunday, what day was 25th July? _____

4. How many Wednesdays are there in September if the last day of the month is a Tuesday? _____

5. What date is the last Friday in April if 25th March is a Thursday? _____

6. How many days after Halloween is Christmas Day? _____

Time questions are often best solved using a table.

For example: Miss Brant leaves for work 30 minutes after Mrs Wilson, who has a 40-minute journey. Mrs Wilson arrives at work at 9.15 a.m. Mrs Sawkins takes 25 minutes to get to work and arrives 10 minutes after Mrs Millman who gets in at 8.30 a.m. Mrs Pepper leaves for work at the same time as Miss Brant and has a journey the same length as Mrs Wilson. What time does Mrs Pepper arrive at work?

- Read all the information. Notice what the question is asking.

- Draw a simple table. Re-read the information. Add to the table any definite facts (shown in black below).

- Work out the rest of the information.

Mrs Sawkins arrives 10 minutes after Mrs Millman, so she arrives at **8.40 a.m.** It takes her 25 minutes to get to work.

To work out when she leaves, take 25 minutes from 8.40 a.m., which is **8.15 a.m.**

Mrs Wilson takes 40 minutes and arrives at 9.15 a.m., so she leaves at **8.35 a.m.**

Miss Brant leaves 30 minutes after Mrs Wilson, so she leaves at **9.05 a.m.**

Mrs Pepper leaves at the same time as Miss Brant, which is **9.05 a.m.** She takes the same time as Mrs Wilson, which is 40 minutes. She arrives at **9.45 a.m.**

	Leaves	**Time taken**	**Arrives**
Miss Brant	9.05 a.m.		
Mrs Wilson	8.35 a.m.	40 mins	9.15 a.m.
Mrs Sawkins	8.15 a.m.	25 mins	8.40 a.m.
Mrs Millman			8.30 a.m.
Mrs Pepper	9.05 a.m.	40 mins	9.45 a.m.

Answer: 9.45 a.m.

Time

1. Pratik, Callum, Prianka and Chrissy all have to be at school by 9 a.m. Pratik catches the 8.20 a.m. bus and arrives at school 10 minutes early. Prianka leaves home at 8.35 a.m. and has a 20-minute walk. Callum leaves home five minutes before Prianka and arrives five minutes after her. Chrissy has a 15-minute cycle ride to school and arrives five minutes before Callum. What time does Chrissy leave home?

   Use the table below to work out your answer.

	Leaves	**Time taken**	**Arrives**
Pratik			
Callum			
Prianka			
Chrissy			

   Answer: _____

2. Salima, Rafi and Emmanuel each take less than two hours to complete their homework. Salima starts at 4.05 p.m., half an hour before Rafi, and finishes at 5.45 p.m. Rafi takes an hour and a half and finishes 20 minutes after Emmanuel, who starts at 5 p.m.
   How long does Emmanuel's homework take?

   Draw your own table using rough paper. Write the answer below.

   Answer: _____

3. Four snails have a race. Brian sets off at 1.25 p.m. and takes 32 minutes to complete the course. Sheldon sets off eight minutes after Brian but completes the course in half the time. Sidney takes 12 minutes longer than Sheldon and finishes at 2.22 p.m. Brenda sets off one minute before Sheldon and completes the course at the same time as Brian.
   Which snail takes the longest to complete the course?

   Draw your own table on a piece of rough paper and write the answer below.

   Answer: _____

In these questions you work out where one thing is in relation to another. Drawing a diagram helps you to use the information given.

For example: Four children are having a picnic. They sit one on each side of a square rug and face the middle. Amita is not sitting next to Mary, who is to the left of Janet. Penny is sitting opposite Janet.
Who is sitting to the right of Penny?

Draw a rectangle to represent the rug. Then put the girls in place, using short forms of their names.

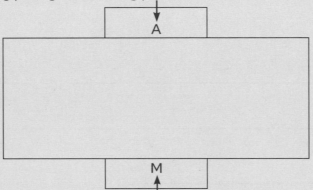

Start by placing Amita in any position and then work from there.

Since Amita is not sitting next to Mary, you know she is sitting opposite her.
So you can put Mary in place.

You also know that Mary is to the left of Janet. The girls are sitting facing the middle, so Janet has to be to the right of Mary.

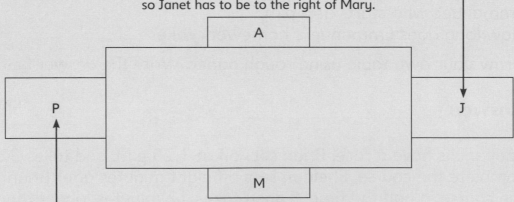

Finally, you can put Penny into the last position.
Now you can see that Mary is sitting to the right of Penny.

Answer: <u>Mary</u>

Hint Play with the information given. If necessary, use **trial and error** until you find the answer.

Use the pictures and lines beneath each question to help you position your answers.

1. Five friends, Barney, Jasper, Harry, Vanessa and Sally, live in a row on Hart Street. Harry lives between Barney and Jasper, who also lives next to Sally. Vanessa lives at one end of the street, next door to Barney.

B =
J =
V =
S =
H =

Who lives at the other end of the street? _____ *Sally* _____

   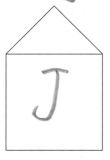 

2. Seven people are in a queue at a bus stop. Mr Dodson is in front of Mrs Bloom but behind Miss Prim. Miss Prim is behind Ms Parker who is behind Mr Ellis. Mr James is behind Mrs Bloom. Mr Maxwell is at the back of the queue.

Who is at the front? ___ MR ELLIS ___

back of the queue   *front of the queue*

Max   James   bloomded   Prim   Park   Ellis

3. Five children, Trevor, Ewan, Melanie, Sue and Paula, are holding hands in a circle, facing inwards. Trevor is holding hands with Melanie and Paula, who is not holding hands with Sue.

Which **two** children is Sue holding hands with? ___ Ewan ___ and ___ paula ___

> **Hint**
> When you make a chart to solve a problem, using shortened forms of names and other details saves you time.

Sorting information

These questions can often be solved by drawing a table.

For example: Jamie, Hannah, Mohammed, Samira and Tamara each like to play sport. Jamie enjoys rugby, football and cricket but does not like swimming. Hannah enjoys netball, football and swimming. Mohammed likes swimming, football, rugby and cricket. Samira likes everything except rugby. Tamara likes football, swimming and cricket.
How many children like swimming?

- Read the information given. Think about the question.

- Draw a table. Use the information to complete it.

	Ru	Fo	Cr	Sw	Ne
Ja	|	|	|	✗	
Ha		|		|	|
Mo	|	|	|	|	
Sa	✗	|	|	|	|
Ta		|	|	|	

Re-read the information, one bit at a time. Fill in the table, using a tally system to note each fact. Check the **Sw** column to see how many children like swimming.

Write your answer on the line.

Answer: 4

1. Five children order an ice-cream sundae each. Max has vanilla, chocolate and strawberry ice-cream in his. Molly has vanilla, fudge and banana. Alex has raspberry ripple, chocolate, banana and a scoop of fudge. Susie has only fudge. Jason has banana, chocolate and fudge. How many children have banana with fudge?

	Ch	Ba	Fu	Va	St	Ra
Ma						
Mo						
Al						
Su						
Ja						

Answer: _____

1. A cat has six kittens. Two of them have brown stripes and white paws. One of them has black paws and no stripes. One is black with three white paws and one black paw. One of them has grey stripes and white paws. One of them is white all over.
How many white paws are there altogether?

Answer: _____

2. A group of friends wrap up warm to play in the snow. Alice wears a pink bobble hat and gloves. Boris wears a scarf and gloves. Cameron wears a hat and a scarf but no gloves. Dottie wears gloves, a scarf and a hat. Ella has a cold so she stays inside. Florence wears a scarf and gloves.
How many children wear at least two items of extra clothing?

Fill in the table to find the answer.

Answer: _____

3. At the Music Academy, pupils can choose up to four different instruments to play. Ajay plays the flute, violin and cello. Leena plays the piano, harp and cello. Amy plays the piano, violin, flute and saxophone. Robert plays the guitar, piano and flute. Yan plays the flute, cello, piano and harp. Beth used to play the harp but now she plays the flute and violin.
How many children play both the piano and flute?

Draw your own table on a piece of rough paper and write the answer below.

Answer: _____

In these questions, you are given one or more true statements. You are then given five more statements, **A** to **E**, which are either true or false. You are asked to **identify** either the one true statement or the one false statement.

For example: Carrots are a root vegetable.
Root vegetables grow underground.

If the above statements in **bold** are true, which **one** of the following statements must also be true?

A. Carrots are orange.

B. All trees have roots.

C. Carrots grow underground.

D. Rabbits like carrots.

E. All vegetables grow underground.

- Read through the first statements, thinking carefully about what they are telling you.

- Next, read statements, **A** to **E**. Compare them to the information given. Decide whether they are true.

- **A.** Carrots are orange. — True, but you **cannot deduce** this from the statements given.

- **B.** All trees have roots. — True, but you **cannot** deduce this from the statements given.

- **C.** Carrots grow underground. — True, and you **can** deduce this from the statements given.

Answer: <u>C</u>

1. Bananas are yellow.

Bananas are a type of fruit.

If the above statements in **bold** are true, which **one** of the following statements is also true?

A. Bananas are tasty.

B. All yellow fruit grows on trees.

C. Bananas are a yellow fruit.

D. All fruit is yellow.

E. Monkeys like bananas.

Answer: _____

I. If the statements shown in **bold** are true, which **one** of the statements listed beneath them is also true?

Eagles are birds of prey.

Birds of prey hunt for their food.

- **A.** Eagles are covered in feathers.
- **B.** Eagles hunt for their food.
- **C.** All birds are eagles.
- **D.** All eagles have wings.
- **E.** Eagles' beaks are yellow.

Answer: _____

2. Cars are a form of transport.

Forms of transport move us from place to place.

- **A.** All forms of transport have wheels.
- **B.** Lorries are forms of transport.
- **C.** Cars move us from place to place.
- **D.** Cars have wheels.
- **E.** Cars carry luggage.

Answer: _____

3. Summer is a season.

There are four seasons.

- **A.** Winter is a season.
- **B.** People eat ice lollies in summer.
- **C.** Summer is hot.
- **D.** Christmas is in winter.
- **E.** Summer is one of four seasons.

Answer: _____

4. Oranges are a type of citrus fruit.

Citrus fruit grows on trees.

- **A.** Orange juice is a type of drink.
- **B.** Orange juice is tasty.
- **C.** Oranges are sticky.
- **D.** Oranges grow on trees.
- **E.** All fruit grows on trees.

Answer: _____

Now test your skills with these practice pages. If you get stuck, go back to pages 58 to 67 for some reminders.

Days and dates

1. Juliette is five months older than Martha, who was born the month before Stella. If Stella was born in June, in which month was Juliette born?

Answer: _____

2. Stanley's older brother, Freddie, went on a trip round the world for 18 months. He returned home in March. In which month did he set off?

Answer: _____

Time

3. Mr Swift is waiting for his flight from London to New York. It was due to depart at 08.35 but is 20 minutes late. The flight takes eight hours. What time does the plane arrive in New York if the time difference is five hours behind the UK?

Answer: _____

4. Jamie's alarm clock goes off at 7.30 a.m. but is five minutes fast. When the alarm goes off, Jamie hits the snooze button. He goes back to sleep for 15 minutes. It takes Jamie 25 minutes to get to school. If he is due in school at 8.45 a.m., how long does he have to get ready and still be on time?

Answer: _____

Position

5. Sashika, Maya, Vitavit, Molly, Sakshay and Joel are queuing for lunch. Maya is in front of Molly but two behind Sakshay who is in front of Joel. Vitavit is not at the back but is further back than Molly. Who is first?

Answer: _____

6. Mrs Morris is sorting out her parcels at the post office. Parcel A weighs 1.5kg, which is 750g heavier than parcel C but 0.25kg lighter than parcel B. Parcel D weighs 150g more than parcel A and 50g less than parcel E. How much does the lightest parcel weigh?

Answer: _____

Sorting information

1. In the burger bar, you can choose any of these toppings: cheese, gherkins, chilli, lettuce, relish and tomatoes. Savi had all the toppings except relish. Bethany and Jordan had cheese, chilli and gherkins on their burgers. Malcolm is allergic to cheese but had everything else apart from chilli. Rhianna had the same as Savi. Angela had a plain burger.
   How many toppings did the children have altogether?

   Answer: _____

2. There are six cars in a car park. Cars **A** and **D** are saloons. Car **E** is a saloon with red stripes and blue doors. Cars **B** and **C** are hatchbacks; one is green and the other is black. Car **F** is a red estate car with black stripes. All the saloons and one of the hatchbacks have a sunroof. All the cars with stripes have air conditioning.
   How many cars have both a sunroof and air conditioning?

   Answer: _____

True statements

If the statements shown in **bold** are true, which **one** of the statements listed beneath them is also true?

3. **Crabs are a type of crustacean.**
   All crustaceans have hard outer shells.
   A. Crabs have pincers.
   B. All crustaceans are crabs.
   C. Crabs have a hard outer shell.
   D. Crabs live in the sea.
   E. Crabs look like spiders.   **Answer:** _____

4. **Paper is often made from wood.**
   Wood comes from trees.
   A. Paper is for writing on.
   B. Books are made out of paper.
   C. Furniture is made out of wood.
   D. Paper can be made from trees.
   E. Paper is white.   **Answer:** _____

Page 4
  1. OZ (+1=O, +2=Z)
  2. BT (−3=B, +3=T)
  3. UF (−1=U, +1=F)
  4. PA (+2=P, −1=A)

Page 5
  1. XZ (+3 +1 +3 +1 +3=XZ)
  2. IJ (+5 +4 +3 +2 +1=IJ)
  3. II (−2 −1 −2 −1 −2=I, −1 −2 −1 −2 −1=I)
  4. SY (−1 −2 −3 −4 −5=S, +1 +2 +3 +4 +5=Y)

These are all **leapfrogging sequences**:

  5. **AC** SU **DF** VX **GI** YA = **JL** (+3)

  6. **PO** DC **ML** BA **JI** ZY = **GF** (−3)

  7. **RO** FD **SP** GE **UR** IG **XU** LJ = **BY** (+1+2+3+4)

  8. **PT** DC **OS** FE **LP** GF **KO** IH = **HL** (−1−3−1−3)

Page 6
  1. Y (both numbered 2)
  2. O (both numbered 12)
  3. T (both numbered 7)
  4. F (both numbered 6)
  5. L (both numbered 12)
  6. H (both numbered 8)
  7. R (both numbered 9)
  8. C (both numbered 3)
  9. V (both numbered 5)
 10. D (both numbered 4)
 11. M (both numbered 13)
 12. P (both numbered 11)

Page 7
  1. IH (numbered 9 8)
  2. EC (numbered 5 3)
  3. KO (numbered 11 12)
  4. AF (numbered 1 6)
  5. IW (numbered 9 4)
  6. OP (numbered 12 11)

Page 8
  1. GI (+3+3)
  2. NQ (−2−2)
  3. MH (+3−2)
  4. IL (+5+4)
  5. OR (−8−8)
  6. TH (+5−5)
  7. VH (+8−2)
  8. MD (−3+4)

Answers

Page 9
1. XLDH
2. HRMT
3. XLZXS
4. KLMB
5. ZMTIB
6. RMHVXG

Page 10
1. YARD
2. DARK
3. DREAM
4. GIRAFFE
5. PLANE
6. ABOUT

Page 11
1. HSFFO (+1 +1 +1 +1 +1)
2. PTHDS (−1 −1 −1 −1 −1)
3. UTHI (+1 +2 +3 +4)
4. EAZOS (−1 −4 −1 −4 −1)
5. VBLDQBH (+3 −1 +3 −1 +3 −1 +3)
6. YMZXP (+5 −5 +5 −5 +5)

Page 12
1. BUSH (−1 −1 −1 −1)
2. RUN (−1 −2 −3)
3. GULL (+2 −2 +2 −2)
4. PLAY (−3 3 3 −3)
5. SISTER (+1 +2 +3 +4 +5 +6)
6. LAUGHTER (−2 +1 −2 +1 −2 +1 −2 +1)

Page 14
1. 3497   8467   3495   8497
   SHIP   CHOP   SHIN   CHIP

   a) 3467
   b) 79584

2. 3419   9841   9517   3519
   SING   GAIN   GONE   SONG

   a) 3551
   b) 89841

3. 1234   4521   4362   1732
   TRAP   PORT   PAIR   TEAR

   a) PART
   b) 172252

Answers

Page 15
1. (pant pan) (band ban) (seem <u>see</u>) (remove last letter)
2. (tram ram) (twin win) (boat <u>oat</u>) (remove first letter)
3. (hop shop) (aid said) (ash <u>sash</u>) (add **s** to the beginning)
4. (many man) (seed see) (lady <u>lad</u>) (remove last letter)
5. (all ball) (ore pore) (ear fear) (add to the beginning of the word the letter that comes next in the alphabet after the first letter of the word; for example, in (**all ball**) the first letter is **a** and the next letter in the alphabet after **a** is **b** – add **b** to **all** to make **ball**)
6. (grown gown) (steal seal) (black <u>back</u>) (remove second letter)
7. (table tale) (tire tie) (bleed <u>bled</u>) (remove third letter)
8. (grain rain) (tread read) (cloud <u>loud</u>) (remove first letter)
9. (bend bed) (sand sad) (burn <u>bun</u>) (remove third letter)
10. (tramp trap) (grind grid) (beard <u>bead</u>) (remove fourth letter)

Page 16
1. (party trap) (stare rats) (liver <u>evil</u>)
2. (tinsel lint) (leaded deal) (denies <u>send</u>)
3. (amused muse) (staked take) (phoned <u>hone</u>)
4. (crawls law) (growls low) (tootle <u>lot</u>)
5. (please slap) (treads drat) (brought <u>grub</u>)
6. (around ran) (apart pat) (abound <u>ban</u>)
7. (trail rat) (though hot) (troop <u>rot</u>)
8. (ground rod) (spoilt pot) (stolen <u>ton</u>)
9. (ambush ham) (inward din) (aghast <u>tag</u>)
10. (adrift rift) (entail tail) (appear <u>pear</u>)

Page 17
1. (bellow low) (maggot got) (barrow <u>row</u>)
2. (juggle leg) (muddle led) (window <u>own</u>)
3. (proper pope) (weaker wake) (fronds <u>fond</u>)
4. (stones nest) (stewed west) (deacon <u>code</u>)
5. (dribble bile) (bramble bale) (whistle <u>tile</u>)
6. (asleep pale) (haunts shun) (instil <u>list</u>)
7. (bottle lot) (middle lid) (toggle <u>log</u>)
8. (doted dot) (metal let) (timed <u>dim</u>)
9. (dented dent) (forest tore) (lunged <u>dung</u>)
10. (denote teen) (handle lean) (galore <u>real</u>)

Page 18
1. (help [hear] pair) (soup [<u>sort</u>] grit)
2. (night [this] sulk) (cream [<u>mare</u>] entry)
3. (magic [aged] mode) (lever [<u>even</u>] line)
4. (shop [save] vane) (pace [<u>plan</u>] alone)
5. (sound [done] lake) (peels [<u>self</u>] leaf)
6. (shower [wash] army) (thumb [<u>moth</u>] open)
7. (hand [hint] site) (lash [<u>lost</u>] moth)
8. (drop [dear] vase) (clap [<u>coal</u>] halo)

Answers

Page 19
1. (melt [test] spot)   (leap [perk] rink)
2. (drop [rope] plea)   (them [heat] arts)
3. (rush [husk] risk)   (leer [rein] pain)
4. (need [dens] soup)   (nets [sent] time)
5. (rattle [right] sigh)   (hanger [heron] hero)
6. (balloon [lands] skid)   (hobbles [bossy] yams)

Page 20
1. GI (I I =G, + I −I)
2. VU (+2=V, +2=U)
3. ZW (−2=Z, −3=W)
4. QJ (−I=Q, +I=J)
5. SA (+I +2 +3 +4 +5=S, +I +2 +3 +4 +5=A)
6. CD (leapfrogging: +2=C, +2=D)
7. KM (+3 +3)
8. KN (letter partners numbered I I 13)
9. VU (letter partners numbered 5 6)
10. TW (+2 +2)
11. ZU (+3 −I)
12. OK (letter partners numbered 12 11)

Page 21
1. OSCOIF (+2 +I +2 +I +2 +I)
2. JMHFGS (−I −I −I −I −I −I)
3. DRIZZLE (letter partners 4 9 9 I I 12 5)
4. LEMON (−I −2 −3 −4 −5)
5. EZOOVB (letter partners 5 I 12 12 5 2)
6. ZMRNZO (letter partners I 13 9 13 I 12)

7. 3451   3463   1487   7463
    THIS   THAT   SHOW   WHAT
    a) 3451
    b) 3467
    c) WASH

8. 6 891   9136   7839   6 873
    MOST   STEM   DOES   MODE
    a) 9136
    b) 68879
    c) SEEDS

Page 22
1. (west wet)   (best bet)   (fast fat)
2. (chain chin)   (grain grin)   (breed bred)
3. (waddle lad)   (little lit)   (meddle led)
4. (matron tram)   (poster stop)   (masher sham)
5. (rampart ramp)   (lantern rant)   (mentors rent)
6. (assures sure)   (redeems seem)   (staring grin)
7. (shut hut)   (grub rub)   (bran ran)
8. (bush bus)   (team tea)   (song son)

Answers

9. (rotten not) (logged <u>dog</u>) (mitten nit)
10. (weed [tore] root) (pies [<u>late</u>] tall)
11. (white [with] trawl) (height [<u>nice</u>] crane)
12. (wand [dawn] dear) (bust [<u>tubs</u>] tent)
13. (bangs [bond] bound) (stale [<u>lies</u>] lines)
14. (flower [slow] houses) (thanks [<u>than</u>] hostels)
15. (windows [chins] coaches) (barrage [<u>spare</u>] whisper)
16. (weep [pray] tray) (door [<u>ring</u>] sing)
17. (table [grab] green) (misty [<u>this</u>] there)
18. (fancy [funny] haiku) (burly [<u>berry</u>] prime)

Page 23
1. (<u>almost</u> always never) (sometimes <u>nearly</u> now)
2. (repeat <u>reply</u> redo) (undo <u>answer</u> refuse)
3. (sturdy detail <u>fragile</u>) (<u>delicate</u> broken grand)
4. (<u>essential</u> essence easy) (hard <u>important</u> difficult)
5. (<u>diminish</u> dessert disaster) (leave <u>reduce</u> increase)
6. (strong <u>weak</u> week) (small <u>frail</u> month)

Page 24
1. <u>ask</u> talk reply annoy <u>question</u>
2. blame <u>defeat</u> assure <u>beat</u> lose
3. hound feline artistic <u>artful</u> <u>crafty</u>
4. <u>destiny</u> detour aloud <u>fate</u> fete
5. class firm soft <u>busy</u> <u>engaged</u>
6. intent <u>impolite</u> distress <u>rude</u> polite
7. <u>bicycle</u> runway station <u>bus</u> wing
8. lamp <u>kitchen</u> shed carpet <u>bedroom</u>

Page 25
1. (<u>begin</u> after stop) (lend land <u>end</u>)
2. (danger <u>despair</u> desperate) (risk <u>hope</u> fear)
3. (<u>mean</u> dark cold) (dim dreary <u>kind</u>)
4. (find <u>full</u> fast) (<u>empty</u> quick found)
5. (healthy <u>include</u> inside) (hungry interior <u>exclude</u>)
6. (movie <u>genuine</u> genius) (real <u>fake</u> film)
7. (perfect pendant <u>new</u>) (brand <u>antique</u> perform)
8. (<u>accept</u> letter gift) (receive thank <u>reject</u>)

Page 26
1. (better, superior) (orange, banana) (<u>mad, sane</u>)
2. (<u>maximum, minimum</u>) (loud, noisy) (father, uncle)
3. (beautiful, pretty) (<u>powerful, feeble</u>) (victory, vanity)
4. (happy, cheerful) (house, garden) (<u>demand, supply</u>)
5. knowledge (wisdom, lazy, legal, question, <u>ignorance</u>)
6. hinder (hamper, annoy, <u>help</u>, hind, honest)
7. encourage (enthusiastic, bored, praise, <u>discourage</u>, disagree)

Answers

Page 27
1. Fish is to (walk, run, <u>swim</u>) as bird is to (trot, <u>fly</u>, jump).
2. Grass is to (long, <u>green</u>, mow) as sand is to (warm, beach, <u>yellow</u>).
3. Uncle is to (old, son, <u>aunt</u>) as sister is to (mother, girl, <u>brother</u>).
4. Eleven is to (<u>twelve</u>, number, two) as four is to (seven, for, <u>five</u>).
5. Teacher is to (bank, park, <u>school</u>) as mechanic is to (car, <u>garage</u>, tip).

Page 28
1. Left is to (leave, <u>right</u>, wrong) as horizontal is to (sun, across, <u>vertical</u>).
2. Attack is to (fight, win, <u>defend</u>) as expand is to (extinct, <u>contract</u>, explain).
3. Fresh is to (<u>stale</u>, edible, air) as humble is to (old, pie, <u>proud</u>).
4. Rush is to (<u>dawdle</u>, jog, skip) as adequate is to (<u>inadequate</u>, less, quad).
5. Clear is to (wash, <u>cloudy</u>, simple) as late is to (eight, cup, <u>early</u>)

Page 29
1. Main is to (horse, <u>mane</u>, least) as sight is to (picture, taste, <u>site</u>).
2. Gardener is to (plants, grow, <u>spade</u>) as painter is to (artist, <u>brush</u>, colour).
3. Stag is to (deer, doe, <u>antlers</u>) as bull is to (<u>horns</u>, calf, field).
4. Taps is to (tops, money, <u>spat</u>) as dab is to (dot, <u>bad</u>, dip).
5. Tree is to (trunk, twigs, <u>roots</u>) as building is to (flat, <u>foundations</u>, home).

Page 30
1. mosquito, cricket (the others are all flowers)
2. organ, guitar (the others are all types of jobs)
3. delight, joy (the others are sad emotions)
4. yacht, canoe (the others are all types of air transport)
5. owl, kestrel (the others are all mammals)
6. lettuce, salad (the others are all types of fruit)

Page 31
1. row (word rhyming with **toe** goes with [paddle, propel] and word rhyming with **cow** goes with [fight, argue])
2. tear (word rhyming with **air** goes with [rip, cut] and word rhyming with **ear** goes with [cry, weep])
3. wound (word with long **oo** sound goes with [injury, hurt] and word rhyming with **sound** goes with [turned, twisted])
4. invalid (word with stress on **in**valid goes with [patient, injured] and word with stress on in**val**id goes with [defunct, obsolete])
5. close (word rhyming with **nose** goes with [shut, cover] and word rhyming with **dose** goes with [near, almost])
6. sow (word rhyming with **so** goes with [plant, cultivate] and word rhyming with **cow** goes with [pig, hog])

Page 32
1. (bargain question <u>baffle</u>) (<u>confuse</u> price answer)
2. (thankful <u>bold</u> afraid) (bald <u>fearless</u> praise)
3. (sweet <u>sour</u> batter) (<u>bitter</u> lemon arrive)
4. (free <u>compliment</u> complex) (<u>flatter</u> argue ignore)
5. (offer <u>beginner</u> began) (<u>novice</u> cause ending)
6. (new <u>ancient</u> ancestor) (<u>modern</u> moderate moreover)
7. (artificial <u>arrange</u> entrance) (fake <u>natural</u> unkind)

Answers

8. (knife bent <u>blunt</u>) (crooked spoon <u>sharp</u>)
9. (cold <u>vague</u> alert) (vanish <u>clear</u> cloudy)
10. (<u>slack</u> slip victory) (win <u>tight</u> victor)
11. Over is to (down, <u>under</u>, out) as enter is to (entrance, into, <u>exit</u>).
12. Racquet is to (noise, <u>badminton</u>, cricket) as stick is to (tree, <u>hockey</u>, glue).
13. Ball is to (cry, <u>bawl</u>, bowl) as seam is to (seal, dress, <u>seem</u>).
14. Fashion is to (clothes, <u>trend</u>, model) as bet is to (<u>wager</u>, bat, win).
15. Clarinet is to (music, <u>wind</u>, play) as drum is to (<u>percussion</u>, sticks, loud).
16. Apple is to (fruit, red, <u>pip</u>) as plum is to (vegetable, juicy, <u>stone</u>).
17. Leap is to (<u>pale</u>, jump, high) as rear is to (<u>rare</u>, rhyme, steer).

Page 33
1. acorn, flower (the others are types of tree)
2. church, temple (the others are educational buildings)
3. fear, delight (the others are anger words)
4. sleep, dream (the others are things you sleep in)
5. doctor, nurse (the others are different words for young people)
6. increase, inflate (the others all mean to get smaller)
7. seal, dolphin (the others are all fish)
8. brother, uncle (the others are all female)
9. joy, jubilation (the others are all to do with sadness)
10. change (the two words **change** are **homonyms**; the two meanings are: 'coins, or money you get back when you pay with more than what is needed' and 'to start being different')
11. wind (the word rhyming with **sinned** goes with [gale, breeze] and the word rhyming with **mind** goes with [turn, rotate])
12. subject (the word with the stress on **sub**ject goes with [topic, lesson] and the word with the stress on sub**ject** goes with [inflict, expose])
13. sewer (the word rhyming with **newer** goes with [drain, effluent] and the word rhyming with **lower** goes with [seamstress, tailor])
14. wave (the two homonyms mean: 'a moving line on the surface of water' and 'a hand gesture that you use to greet a friend')
15. star (the two homonyms mean: 'a bright object seen in the sky at night' and 'a very famous person')
16. case (the two homonyms mean: 'an incident that is investigated by lawyers' and 'a box to keep or carry things in')
17. land (the two homonyms mean: 'to come back to the land after being on a plane or a ship' and 'the part of the earth not covered by the sea')
18. number (the word with the **b** sounded goes with [figure, numeral] and the word with a silent **b** goes with [duller, soothed])

Page 34
1. e (spine, eyes)
2. m (stream, meat)
3. t (greet, tomb)
4. p (soup, piglet)
5. n (town, neck)
6. a (sofa, apple)

Answers

Page 35
1. k (walk, king, milk, kite)
2. p (clap, pine, leap, pound)
3. e (wave, eat, time, earth)
4. g (sting, gnat, drag, glare)
5. n (train, nought, grin, near)
6. l (mill, lake, steal, live)
7. l (shovel, lost, towel, lower)
8. h (month, high, youth, hand)

Page 36
1. s (pray, seat)
2. r (bought, drown)
3. c (lamp, chill)
4. t (rust, burnt)
5. r (band, heard)
6. g (rain, began)

Page 37
1. HAT (that) *or* HIS (this)
2. SIT (visit)
3. LIP (slipped)
4. ANT (wants)
5. HEN (when)
6. OWL (howled)
7. RAN (grandma)
8. PEN (spent)
9. ICE (rice)
10. LOP (slope)

Page 38 *Check that you have used **horizontal** lines to mark your answers as shown below.*

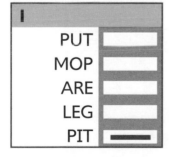 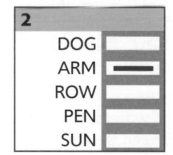 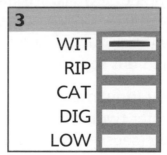

1. PIT (hospital)
2. ARM (alarmed)
3. WIT (switch)

Page 40
1. Have you seen the<u>m eat</u> their meal yet? (meat)
2. My uncle had hi<u>s own</u> aeroplane. (sown)
3. You need a war<u>m ove</u>n for baking bread. (move)
4. The dreadful storm was a weat<u>her d</u>isaster. (herd)
5. I like to jo<u>g one</u> mile each day. (gone)
6. Nervously, the competitor<u>s ent</u>ered the ring. (sent)
7. Sally scored <u>the m</u>ost points in the test. (them)

Answers

8. He was the fir<u>st o</u>pponent to cross the line. (stop)
9. There was a sud<u>den t</u>hunder crash. (dent)
10. New employees bring ne<u>w idea</u>s. (wide)
11. Some child<u>ren t</u>hink teachers know everything. (rent)
12. The views <u>alter</u> depending on the light. (salt)
13. Some seeds never germinate but the<u>se alwa</u>ys do. (seal)
14. Felt tips for sale – fi<u>ve in</u> a packet! (vein)
15. Reaching the peak would <u>be a</u> tough climb. (beat)
16. The aging <u>lady</u> climbed out of the carriage. (glad)
17. I a<u>m a kee</u>n swimmer but I prefer tennis. (make)
18. Hav<u>e a ch</u>ocolate if you'd like one! (each)
19. My T-shirt had a long <u>rip</u> down the back. (grip)
20. All member<u>s of t</u>he club train daily. (soft)

Page 41
1. (can <u>key</u> car) (band <u>board</u> bored) (keyboard)
2. (<u>puff</u> poor peer) (on <u>in</u> out) (puffin)
3. (by but <u>be</u>) (<u>hind</u> hound hand) (behind)
4. (<u>end</u> and under) (<u>less</u> loss lass) (endless)
5. (about <u>over</u> even) (near give <u>take</u>) (overtake)
6. (paint path <u>pass</u>) (<u>port</u> part pant) (passport)

Page 42
1. (tar <u>bar</u> car) (grin <u>gain</u> ten) (bargain)
2. (<u>post</u> most pine) (<u>age</u> and or) (postage)
3. (is us <u>as</u>) (queen <u>king</u> prince) (asking)
4. (yes <u>not</u> all) (is in <u>ice</u>) (notice)
5. (up <u>so</u> it) (<u>lid</u> led lad) (solid)
6. (<u>he</u> him her) (row air <u>art</u>) (heart)
7. (miss <u>to</u> let) (<u>ward</u> take end) (toward)
8. (<u>sign</u> train grow) (ape <u>post</u> aim) (signpost)
9. tear <u>bar</u> out) (round key <u>row</u>) (barrow)
10. (and out <u>so</u>) (at <u>on</u> off) (soon)

Page 43
1. day (daytime, daylight, daydream, daybreak)
2. water (waterfall, waterfront, waterbed, waterwheel)
3. sea (seashell, seashore, seaweed, seasick)
4. sun (sunset, sunshine, sundown, suntan)
5. back (backpack, backward, backhand, background)
6. air (aircraft, airport, airbrush, airship)

Page 44
1. y (army, your, play, yacht)
2. g (clog, goal, hang, give)
3. e (mate, easy, wine, even)
4. k (blink, knit, track, king)
5. d (flood, drive, round, damp)
6. p (flap, pansy, steep, piano)
7. l (metal, liver, growl, loose)
8. w (draw, windy, flaw, weary)

9. e (dram, weed)
10. s (have, barns)
11. e (cram, tripe)
12. i (nave, lied)
13. l (peat, model)
14. u (cold, bound)
15. v (lied. valley)
16. h (torn, booth)

Page 45
1. MAN (manage)
2. LID (slide)
3. SAY (essay)
4. CAN (candle)
5. OUR (pouring)
6. PIN (spinning)
7. TIN (tinsel)
8. It's time to gather the crops. (toga)
9. She smiled her brightest smile. (herb)
10. Sweep up the leaves and rubbish, please. (sand)
11. Laugh and smile every day! (hand)
12. He arrived late and Mum was cross. (hear)
13. It's important not to waste a minute! (team)
14. (up count sing) (out down in) (countdown)
15. (door roof window) (letter out man) (doorman)
16. (round under through) (above below about) (roundabout)
17. (head neck fear) (loss list lace) (necklace)
18. (about over even) (near give take) (overtake)
19. (is be as) (an up off) (bean)

Page 46
1. 23 (+3)
2. 10 (−5 −4 −3 −2 −1)
3. 24 (+2 +3 +2 +3 +2)
4. 3 (−3)
5. 16 (−2 −3 −1 −2 −3 −1)
6. 36 (+6 +5 +4 +3 +2)

Page 47
1. 32 (×2)
2. 10 (÷2)
3. 81 (×3)
4. 25 (÷2)
5. 600 (×5 ×4 ×3 ×2)
6. 6 (÷2)
7. 1200 (×5 ×4 ×3 ×2)
8. 5 (÷6 ÷5 ÷4 ÷3)
9. 567 (×3)
10. 0.12 (÷10)

Answers

Page 48
1. 9 (leapfrogging, starting on 3, +2 each time)
2. 15 (leapfrogging, starting on 30, −5 each time)
3. 13 (adding the two previous numbers: 5 + 8)
4. 65 (adding the two previous numbers: 25 + 40)
5. 95 (doubling the amount added each time: +3 +6 +12 +24 +48, *or* doubling the number, then adding 1: 2×2=4+1=5, 2×5=10+1=11, 2×11=22+1=23, etc.)
6. 15 (leapfrogging, starting on 120, ÷2 each time)
7. 156 (adding the two previous numbers: 60 + 96)
8. 438 (doubling the amount added each time: +14 +28 +56 +112 +224, *or* doubling the number and then adding 10: 2×4=8+10=18, 2×18=36+10=46, 2×46=92+10=102, etc.)
9. 9 (leapfrogging, starting on 1, +2 each time)
10. 8 (leapfrogging, starting on 2, +2 each time)

Page 49
1. 343 (cube numbers: 3^3, 4^3, 5^3, 6^3, 7^3)
2. 100 (square numbers: 6^2 7^2 8^2 9^2 10^2)
3. 49 (square numbers: 3^2 4^2 5^2 6^2 7^2)
4. 8 (cube numbers: 6^3, 5^3, 4^3, 3^3, 2^3)
5. 16 (adding the two previous numbers: 6 + 10)
6. 15 (doubling the amount added each time: +2 +4 +8 +16 +32, *or* doubling the number and then adding 1: 2×1=2+1=3, 2×3=6+1=7, 2×7=14+1=15, etc.)
7. 30 (leapfrogging, starting on 40, −10 each time)
8. 5 (adding the two previous numbers: 11 − 6 = 5, *or* 5 + 6 = 11)

Page 50
1. E (16)
2. E (40)
3. A (3)
4. C (48)
5. B (168)
6. A (50)

Page 51
1. 2
2. 5
3. 7
4. 4
5. 2
6. 8
7. 4
8. 8
9. 0
10. 4

Answers

Page 52 **1.** 15
         2. 2
         3. 2
         4. 8
         5. 23
         6. 90

Page 53 **1.** 24 ($\times$)
         2. 20 ($+$)
         3. 19 ($-$)
         4. 15 ($\times$)
         5. 4 ($\div$)
         6. 56 ($\times$)
         7. 8 ($\div$)
         8. 41 ($-$)

Page 55 **1.** 48 (a $\times$ b, then $\times$2)
         2. 27 (a + b, then +1)
         3. 14 (b − a, then −1)
         4. 12 (a + b, then ÷2)
         5. 14 (a ÷ b, then +10)
         6. 15 (b − a, then −1)
         7. 17 (a ÷ b, then +b)
         8. 61 (a + b, then −8)

Page 56 **1.** 42 (+7)
         2. 192 ($\times$2)
         3. 36 (−12)
         4. 64 (all square numbers: the answer is 8^2)
         5. 38 (+2 +4 +6 +8 +10)
         6. 36 (leapfrogging, +9: 9, 18, 27, 36)
         7. 159 (doubling the number added each time: +5 +10 +20 +40 +80)
         8. 156 (adding the two previous numbers: 60 + 96 = 156)
         9. 30 (÷2)
     10. 125 (all cube numbers: the answer is 5^3)
     11. E (14)
     12. C (28)
     13. A (3)
     14. D (15)
     15. B (39)
     16. A (65)

Answers

Page 57
1. 5
2. 7
3. 36
4. 3
5. 2
6. 2
7. 39
8. 3
9. 97
10. 3
11. 42 (a × b)
12. 33 (a + b)
13. 47 (a − b)
14. 11 (a ÷ b)
15. 38 (b − a)
16. 80 (a ÷ b, then ×10)
17. 27 (a × b, then −1)
18. 30 (a + b, then −10)
19. 71 (a + b + b)
20. 46 (a − b, then ×2)

Page 58
1. Friday
2. November
3. Wednesday
4. Sunday
5. March
6. February

Page 59
1. Saturday
2. Five (on 2nd, 9th, 16th, 23rd and 30th March)
3. Wednesday
4. Four (3rd, 10th, 17th and 24th September)
5. 30th April
6. 55 days (30 in November + 25 in December)

Page 61
1. 8.40 a.m.

Make a table using the information you are given.

Name	Leaves	Time taken	Arrives
Pratik	8.20 a.m.		8.50 a.m.
Callum	8.30 a.m.		9.00 a.m.
Prianka	8.35 a.m.	20 mins	8.55 a.m.
Chrissy	8.40 a.m.	15 mins	8.55 a.m.

2. 45 minutes

Make a table using the information you are given.

Name	Starts	Time taken	Finishes
Salima	4.05 p.m.		5.45 p.m.
Rafi	4.35 p.m.	1hr 30 mins	6.05 p.m.
Emmanuel	5 p.m.	45 mins	5.45 p.m.

3. Brian

Make a table using the information you are given.

Name	Starts	Time taken	Finishes
Brian	1.25 p.m.	32 mins	1.57 p.m.
Sheldon	1.33 p.m.	16 mins	
Sidney		28 mins	2.22 p.m.
Brenda	1.32 p.m.	25 mins	1.57 p.m.

Page 63 1. Sally

2. Mr Ellis

back of the queue   *front of the queue*

<u>Mr Ma</u>   <u>Mr Ja</u>   <u>Mrs Bl</u>   <u>Mr Do</u>   <u>Miss Pr</u>   <u>Ms Pa</u>   <u>Mr El</u>

3. Ewan and Melanie

Page 64 1. Three children (Molly, Alex and Jason)

*Your completed table should look like this. To answer the question, you count the number of children who have **both** banana **and** fudge.*

	Ch	Ba	Fu	Va	St	Ra
Ma	I			I	I	
Mo		I	I	I		
Al	I	I	I			I
Su			I			
Ja	I	I	I			

Answers

Page 65 **1.** 19 white paws

Remember that each kitten has four paws.

2 kittens with brown stripes and white paws = 2 × 4 = 8 white paws
1 kitten with 1 black and 3 white paws = 3 white paws
1 kitten with grey stripes and white paws = 4 white paws
1 kitten with white all over = 4 white paws

8 + 3 + 4 + 4 = 19

(A sixth kitten has black paws and no white ones at all.)

2. Five children

Make a table and count the number of rows with two or more tally marks.

	Ha	Gl	Sc
A	|	|	
B		|	|
C	|		|
D	|	|	|
E			
F		|	|

3. Three children (Amy, Robert and Yan)

*Make a table and count the number of rows with tally marks in **both** the flute **and** the piano columns.*

	Fl	Vi	Ce	Pi	Ha	Sa	Gu
Aj	|	|	|				
L			|	|	|		
Am	|	|		|		|	
R	|			|			|
Y	|		|	|	|		
B	|	|					

Page 66 **1.** C

Page 67 **1.** B
           2. C
           3. E
           4. D

Answers

Page 68 **1.** December

Juliette	Born five months earlier than May (when Martha was born) = December
Stella	Born in June
Martha	Born one month earlier than June (the month before Stella) = May

2. September

Work out what month it would have been 18 months earlier than March.
March less 12 months = March. Take away another six months = September.

3. 11.55

Plane departs at 08.35 plus 20 minutes = 08.55.
Flight arrives 08.55 plus 8 hours = 16.55 UK time.
16.55 minus five hours = 11.55.

4. 40 minutes

The alarm clock goes off at 7.30 a.m. minus five minutes = 7.25 a.m.
Jamie sleeps until 7.25 a.m. plus 15 minutes = 7.40 a.m.
He could get to school at 7.40 a.m. plus 25 minutes = 8.05 a.m.
He doesn't have to be there until 8.45 a.m.
So he has 8.45 minus 8.05 = 40 minutes to get ready.

5. Sakshay

The order of the people in the queue is as follows:

Back of queue					Front of queue
Sashika	Vitavit	Molly	Maya	Joel	Sakshay

6. 750g (parcel C)

It is helpful at the start to convert the weights given in kilograms into grams.
Then all the weights are in the same units.

A	1.5kg = 1500g
B	1500g plus 0.25kg (250g) = 1750g
C	C = 1500g minus 750g = 750g
D	1500g plus 150g = 1650g
E	1650g plus 50g = 1700g

Page 69 **1.** 20

Make a table and then count all the tally marks to find the answer.

	che	ghe	chi	let	rel	tom
Sa	|	|	|	|	X	|
Be	|	|	|			
Jo	|	|	|			
Ma	X	|	X	|	|	|
Rhi	|	|	|	|	X	|
Ang	X	X	X	X	X	X

2. One (car E)

Make a table and then count the number of cars that have tally marks in both of the last two columns (sunroof and air con).

	saloon	hatch	estate	stripe	door col	sunroof	air con
A	|					|	
B		|				Either B or C has a sunroof |	
C		|					
D	|					|	
E	|			|	|	|	|
F			|	|			|

3. C

4. D

Tips for tests

These tips will be useful as you prepare for school tests, such as the 11+, and for practice tests that you do at school or at home.

1. Always read the questions carefully.

2. When doing practice papers, check the format of the real test. It could be in the standard format or the multiple choice format and it is a good idea to do practice papers of the right kind.

3. Don't just circle the first answer you see that you think is right. Check every multiple choice answer option to make sure you have definitely picked the right one.

4. Mark your answer clearly and make sure you know what to do if you make a mistake. In some tests you are asked to rub out an incorrect answer. In others you are asked to cross it out.

5. Don't spend too long on one question. If you are finding it difficult, put a circle around the question number and then come back to it at the end if you have time. By putting a circle around the number you'll be able to see easily which ones you need to go back to.

6. If you finish before the end, **go back and check your answers**, especially any you weren't completely sure about. You'd be surprised how many people make silly mistakes or even leave out whole pages of questions by mistake.

7. If there is a question you really can't answer, you might as well have a guess. With multiple choice answers, it is worth a try. You never know, you might guess the right answer.

8. When you are doing a practice test, ask an adult to time you and let you know when you are half way through the test – and when you have five minutes left. This will help you to become more aware of how quickly you need to work.

Tips for revision

1. Practice is the key. The more you do, the better you will get.

2. When revising for a test, allocate more time to practising the question types you are weaker in as this will help you to improve.

3. Since timing is important for tests, develop your sense of time by asking an adult to time you while you attempt fun challenges, such as 'How many times can I write my name in one minute?' or 'How many jumps can I do in 30 seconds?'

4. Make sure that you have a quiet place to work, without any distractions.

In order to speed up your answering of maths questions, learn key mathematical facts such as times tables, division facts, addition and subtraction facts to 20. Schofield & Sims has a range of books that will help you. Ask your adult helper to check the website **www.schofieldandsims.co.uk**

Index and glossary